WORLD
ON
FIRE

HANNAH ANDERSON / JADA EDWARDS / RACHEL GILSON
ASHLEY MARIVITTORI GORMAN / JASMINE HOLMES / REBECCA MCLAUGHLIN
JEN POLLOCK MICHEL / MARY WILEY / ELIZABETH WOODSON

WORLD ON FIRE

WALKING IN THE WISDOM
OF CHRIST WHEN EVERYONE'S
FIGHTING ABOUT EVERYTHING

B&H
PUBLISHING
NASHVILLE, TENNESSEE

Published by B&H Publishing Group
Nashville, Tennessee

Dewey Decimal Classification: 226.93
Subject Heading: BEATITUDES / SERMON ON THE MOUNT /
SOCIAL PROBLEMS

It is the Publisher's goal to minimize disruption caused by techni-
cal errors or invalid websites. While all links are active at the time
of publication, because of the dynamic nature of the internet, some
web addresses or links contained in this book may have changed and
may no longer be valid. B&H Publishing Group bears no responsibility for the continuity or content of the external site, nor for that of
subsequent links. Contact the external site for answers to questions
regarding its content.

Cover design by B&H Publishing Group.
Cover illustration CSA Images/gettyimages.
Interior icons by bluebright/vectorstock.

1 2 3 4 5 6 • 25 24 23 22 21

CONTENTS

Chapter 1   **World on Fire**   1
             Hannah Anderson

Chapter 2   **Poor in Spirit and in the Right Kingdom**   13
             Rebecca McLaughlin

Chapter 3   **Mourning Sin in a World That Forgets It**   29
             Elizabeth Woodson

Chapter 4   **Meekness in a World of Pride**   43
             Hannah Anderson

Chapter 5   **Holistic Righteousness in a World That's Selective**   55
             Jada Edwards

Chapter 6   **Mercy in a World of Scrooges**   69
             Ashley Marivittori Gorman

Chapter 7   **A Singular Focus in an Unfocused World**   87
             Jasmine Holmes

Chapter 8   **Making True Peace in a World of False Peace**   101
             Rachel Gilson

Chapter 9   **Persecution in a World of Comfort**   117
             Mary Wiley

CONTENTS

Chapter 10   **Salt and Light in a World of Decay
             and Darkness**   131
             Jen Pollock Michel

About the Authors   143

Chapter 1

WORLD ON FIRE

Hannah Anderson

Consider how a small fire sets ablaze a large forest.
And the tongue is a fire. The tongue, a world of
unrighteousness . . . sets the course of life on fire.
—James 3:5–6

"I just don't know what to believe anymore. I mean, who can you trust?"

Her face fell as she said the words. She wrapped her hands around the cup of coffee and slumped back into her chair. I didn't say anything in response because there wasn't anything to say. Words felt unequal to the moment. So instead, we sat in silence, feeling the weight of it all.

The past year had brought a world of suffering and chaos. A global pandemic shuttered churches, schools, and businesses and left families mourning lost loved ones. Hurricanes pummeled the coasts while wildfires raged across millions of acres. Racial hatred, once again emboldened, emerged from the shadows in all its grotesque forms. Millions found themselves un- and under-employed while others worked under the threat of professional consequences for stepping out of line or voicing unpopular opinions. To top it all off, a fraught election cycle climaxed in a deadly attack on the seat of government while elected officials were in the process of governing.

And it all was delivered via the screens that sat on the table between us, just inches from our fingertips. Each update, each statistic, each poll, each political scandal had flashed across those small devices—devices that we somehow believed we needed to carry with us everywhere. Like my friend, I too found myself guarded and wary, fluctuating between anger, anxiety, and ironically enough, loneliness. I walked on eggshells, uncertain of what I could say and to whom. And despite my best efforts, I'd invariably offend someone, miscommunicating with friends and family. Then I'd watch helplessly as the bonds that had once held us close strained under the stress of it all, threatening to break for good if we couldn't perfectly agree on everything.

It felt like the world as we had known it had gone up in flames.

How Great a Fire

When I think of a raging fire, I think of my father-in-law who worked as a forester for four decades. Throughout his career, he managed hundreds of acres, partnered with landowners to steward and cultivate their properties, and battled the forest fires that would inevitably break out. In fact, my husband tells of a childhood punctuated by "fire season"—a period of several months in spring and fall when forest fires are common due to environmental factors like dryness, bare trees, and high winds. During fire season, my father-in-law couldn't travel outside a prescribed radius, needing instead to stay close to his work truck, ever ready, ever vigilant, should a fire break out.

Because all it took was one spark. One match, one flame could set the hills ablaze.

In many ways, this cultural moment is a kind of "fire season" with conditions just right for fire to break out. Technological advances (while in many ways a blessing) have also brought significant challenges and even dangers. Where we once had too little information, we now have too much. It's impossible for one person to sort through all the data points, opinions, and facts, so we often end up relying on other people to interpret the information for us, telling us what we should and shouldn't think.

Add to this the fact that social media is designed to reward interaction. Ever wonder why clickbait is so popular or why you only see certain posts in your time line? By prioritizing content that is likely to grab our attention, social media algorithms keep us active and engaged. Unfortunately, they also create information silos that stoke division and tribalism.

But the challenge is greater than just identifying our biases or making sure we follow folks on both sides of an issue. Technology has also given us the ability to manipulate images and manufacture data so that it's increasingly difficult to know if what we're reading is factual or not. We have moved far beyond the question of "How can I get knowledge or information?" and find ourselves asking "How can I know this knowledge or information is *true*?" One study reveals that answering this question might be harder than we'd think, as it found that false information spread six times faster than accurate information.[1] Forget the information age—we're living in the disinformation age.

All of this makes for a combustible environment, rife for disagreement, conflict, and fragmentation. But fires don't break out just because conditions are right. They must be lit, if only by accident.[2] So what was the spark that sets this tinder alight? What is the spark that has set our world on fire?

The Spark

The 2020 documentary *The Social Dilemma* traces the effects of the digital age on individuals and communities, highlighting how social media has led to a breakdown of trust and larger social instability.

---

[1] Peter Dizikes, "Study: On Twitter, False News Travels Faster than True Stories," MIT News, March 8, 2018, http://news.mit.edu/2018/study-twitter-false-news-travels-faster-true-stories-0308.

[2] While arson is suspected in several of the 2020 wildfires, the El Dorado fire was traced back to a gender reveal party in which an expectant couple had set off fireworks to celebrate.

In it, computer scientist and design ethicist Tristan Harris makes an important observation: technology itself is not necessarily the threat.

"We're all looking out for the moment when technology would overwhelm human strengths and intelligence," Harris says. He goes on:

> When is it going to . . . replace our jobs, be smarter than humans? But there's this much earlier moment when technology exceeds and overwhelms **human weaknesses**. This point being crossed is at the root of addiction, polarization, radicalization, outrage-ification, vanity-ification, the entire thing. . . . It's technology's ability to bring out the worst in society and the worst in society brings the existential threat.[3]

In other words, while technology may create the conditions, the spark that sets the world on fire is . . . us.

Although he probably doesn't realize it, Harris is echoing what the apostle James knew in the first century. In James 3:14, he writes that "bitter envy and selfish ambition" fuel "disorder and every vile practice" (v. 16). In the next chapter he says it this way: "What is the source of wars and fights among you? Don't they come from your passions that wage war within you?" (4:1). Bitterness. Envy. Vile practices. Wars and fights among us. Sounds a lot like the present moment, doesn't it? But just a few verses prior, James also says this: "How great a forest is set ablaze by such a small fire! And the tongue is a fire, a world of unrighteousness . . . setting on fire the entire course of life" (3:5–6 ESV).

According to James, *we* are the ones who light the fires with our knee-jerk reactions and our constant need to be right. But James isn't addressing simply what we *say*. He's addressing the deeper realities of our heart, because what we say, write, and profess reveal what's happening within us. We wage war on the outside because we have

---

[3] Jeff Orlowski, dir. *The Social Dilemma*, Exposure Labs, 2020, https://www.netflix.com/title/81254224 [emphasis added].

passions waging war on the *inside*. "The source" of all the fighting, of all the fires, isn't "out there" with some person or group we disagree with. It is "in here." The spark is the sinful passions and desires within the human heart, both yours and mine. Our mouths simply give them voice. As Jesus put it in Luke 6:45, "[the] mouth speaks from the overflow of the heart."

The danger isn't simply that we struggle to know and say what's true, but that too many of us don't want the truth in the first place. The problem is that we're interacting with other people from fleshly hearts that are full of "bitter envy and selfish ambition." Technology has created a combustible environment, sure. It has made it easier for us to be terrible to each other. And that is something to mourn and resist (many tech-experts will tell you that was done on purpose). But what James holds up in front of us is this: the desire to be terrible in these ways, regardless of environment, has always been smoldering within us. Our environment can only fan the flame of destruction because the flame is there in the first place.

Fire Safety and Heavenly Wisdom

While my father-in-law's work demanded vigilance during fire season, he spent the rest of the year reducing the risk of fire through things like reforestation, prescribed burns, and teaching fire safety to the larger public. (When the moment called for it, he wasn't above donning a Smokey the Bear costume to remind folks that "Only you can prevent forest fires!")

The idea behind fire safety is simple: you can't control the elements. You can't control how much rain will come and how dry the forest will be. But you can control *your* behavior. You can choose to make wise choices about when and where you start fires and whether you're careless with matches. You can conduct yourself with wisdom instead of foolishness.

After warning us about how the tongue can set the world on fire, James asks this question: "Who among you is wise and understanding?

By his good conduct he should show that his works are done in the gentleness *that comes from wisdom*" (3:13, emphasis added). And with this, James sets up a contrast between those who pursue wisdom and those who indulge their sinful tendencies. "But if you have bitter envy and selfish ambition in your heart," he continues, "don't boast and deny the truth. Such wisdom does not come down from above but is earthly, unspiritual, demonic" (3:14–15). Simply put, there are those who fight the fires and those who start them. There are those who seek heavenly wisdom and those who act out of earthly wisdom.

So what would this heavenly wisdom look like? How can we tell the difference between the wisdom that is from above and "wisdom" that is simply enabling, excusing, and encouraging our human weaknesses and fleshly desires?

First, heavenly wisdom is counterintuitive. Biblical wisdom has a way of confusing us at first because it challenges the assumptions that emerge from our sin nature. This is what Proverbs 14:12 means when it says that "There is a way that seems right to a person, but its end is the way to death." Our instinct or gut feeling about how to respond to a situation or issue is not enough—neither is "feeling peace" or a "lack of peace." Instead, we are pursuing the "renewing" of our minds (Rom. 12:2). We are inviting God's Word and God's Spirit to make us into the image of God's Son, to conform our thoughts and words and deeds to his likeness. So, as we explore what wisdom looks like in these times, expect to be surprised. Welcome the experience of feeling challenged. Why? Because this is exactly what the Scripture tells us will happen when we're being changed.

Second, heavenly wisdom is knowable to all who seek it. Wisdom is not the exclusive property of a select few who have discovered a secret memo, a secret meaning, or a secret cabal. In fact, in James 1:5, the Scripture invites "*any* of you" who lack wisdom to come to God, promising that he will give it to all truly seeking him. The challenge of wisdom is not that only a few can "know" what is true or real. The challenge is that wisdom requires hard things of us. It disrupts and confronts us, so many of us simply choose to look away from it. We don't want to look at "the source" of the wars being waged among us, namely, our own sinful passions and desires. We resist the invitation because doing so would also mean admitting that we are part of the problem. To face our inner arsonist and drag it into the light would take an enormous amount of both courage and humility. This is why James warns us that coming to God for wisdom will require singleness of heart. Anyone can come to God for wisdom; but only those humble enough to believe that God's ways are better than our own will find it.

Third, heavenly wisdom is countercultural. Those seeking the heavenly wisdom are seeking the "narrow way" that leads to life and flourishing—a narrow way that many other people won't necessarily understand (Matt. 7:14). Even other Christians. Even their fellow citizens. In fact, heavenly wisdom will likely disrupt the status quo because it seeks the kingdom of God rather than a kingdom on this earth. In this way, heavenly wisdom challenges both our personal assumptions and our cultural and social assumptions. So don't be surprised if, in pursuing heavenly wisdom, you find yourself swimming against the current in unexpected ways. Don't be surprised when what you once thought to be *common* wisdom turns out not to be wisdom at all.

Fourth, heavenly wisdom points to the gospel. Rather than reinforcing our sense of righteousness and self-reliance, heavenly wisdom challenges us while leading us to repentance and grace. After all, if Jesus is the wisdom of God (1 Cor. 1:24), his ways, works, and words will align, teaching us how to live out the gospel in practical ways. Even more, lives based on heavenly wisdom will bolster our claims that Jesus himself is the way, the truth, and the life. Living in foolishness, on the other hand, will undermine our gospel witness because the disconnect between what we say and what we do will be glaringly obvious to anyone watching. Consider how Paul calls out the partiality and segregation that was occurring in the church at Galatia—when certain Christians separated themselves from their brothers and sisters. He says that "their conduct was not in step with the truth of the gospel" (Gal. 2:14 ESV). The way they were mistreating those of a different background reflected earthly values and earthly wisdom.

Heavenly wisdom, on the other hand, calls believers to behavior that embodies Christ and his cross.

And finally, heavenly wisdom seeks union and reconciliation. Listen again to the words of James: "But the wisdom that is from above is first pure, then peaceable, gentle, open to reason, full of mercy and good fruits, impartial and sincere. And a harvest of righteousness is sown in peace by those who make peace" (3:17–18 ESV). The goal of heavenly wisdom is not simply to separate those who are right from those who are wrong. The goal of heavenly wisdom is to identify and heal the brokenness in our midst. The goal of heavenly wisdom is *reconciliation*. And while it's true that some may resist that reconciliation, those seeking heavenly wisdom will not. Those truly seeking to live like Christ understand that the goal of the gospel is reconciling us to God and each other.

Facing a Choice

Sitting across the table from my friend that morning, I felt helpless. And if I'm honest, I've felt that way many days since. The problems are too large, the divides too great. The cultural environment around us is dry kindle, rife with misinformation and manipulation. Any little spark will light it ablaze and engulf the whole.

But the truth is that we aren't hopeless or helpless. We may not be able to change what's happening around us, but we can change who we are in the midst of it. We can respond to the invitation to move toward heavenly wisdom, asking the Holy Spirit to make us people who learn to tame the fire.

For Christians, cultivating this heavenly wisdom cannot be separated from Jesus of Nazareth who the Scripture declares to be the wisdom of God himself.[4] For us, becoming wise ultimately means

---

[4] According to John 1, Jesus of Nazareth is not simply a wise prophet but the embodiment of wisdom itself. He is the *Logos* or thought of God. First Corinthians 1:24 also calls Christ the power and "wisdom of God."

becoming mature disciples of Jesus who learn to love God with our whole heart, *mind*, and strength and our neighbor as ourselves (Mark 12:30). Or as Philippians 2:5 puts it, becoming wise means having "the mind" of Christ—learning to think and respond and act as he would.

So through the next nine chapters, we're going to explore heavenly wisdom as Jesus presents it in the Sermon on the Mount. Focusing specifically on the Beatitudes, we'll see how Jesus leads his followers to embrace a way of living in the world that leads to life and peace and blessing. The chapters and topics will be as varied as the writers themselves, and hopefully we'll all learn more because of multiple perspectives.

But one thing will be consistent, whether we're thinking about what it means to be poor in spirit or how our good works give glory to the Father, instead of taking us out of the fire, the wisdom of Jesus teaches us how to tame it—starting with our *own* hearts first. Instead of changing our circumstances, this heavenly wisdom changes *who we are within them*. And above all else, this heavenly wisdom will point us back to the One who is the hope of the world.

Application

Looking In

James tells us that the division and strife we experience externally begins internally, with "bitter envy and selfish ambition." In order to pursue peace with others, we must honestly assess our own hearts and the role we play in the larger conflict.

1. How have your relationships shifted over the last few years? In what ways have they gotten better and in what ways have they become strained? Do you view social media and the internet as contributing to the change?

2. How would you describe the larger social and political climate? Where are you seeing fragmentation and division? Before reading this chapter, who did you think was primarily responsible for this?

3. Do you agree with Tristan Harris's assessment that technology has "exceed[ed] and overwhelm[ed] human weaknesses"? Do you find your own emotions and responses harder to control in the present climate? Do you find yourself either "walking on eggshells" or "flying off the handle"?

4. Share a time when your responses or actions accelerated an already difficult situation. Looking back, what was happening inside you? Why did you respond the way you did and what would you change if you could do it over again?

Looking Up

Thankfully, James also tells us that God welcomes all who come to him for wisdom. According to James 1:5, he "gives to all generously and ungrudgingly" and does not belittle or condemn us in our weakness.

1. As you consider you own reactions and responses, where do you find yourself "lacking wisdom"? When do you most feel your need for heavenly wisdom?

2. Read James 1:5–6. What do you think it means that those who come to God for wisdom must come "in faith without doubting"? How does being "double-minded" hinder our ability to receive wisdom from God (v. 8)?

3. We often think of Jesus in his role as the Redeemer or Savior of the world. How does it change your understanding of who he is to also think of him as "the wisdom of God"?

4. The goal of the gospel is to reconcile us to God and each other. How does pursuing wisdom continue the work that Christ began at the cross?

Looking Out

James also contrasts earthly wisdom and heavenly wisdom, showing how they affect our relationships and communities. In the Sermon on the Mount, Jesus does something similar with the phrase, "You have heard it said, but I say unto you." With these words, he draws people's attention to the fact that the wisdom of God surpasses and challenges "common wisdom."

1. Name a commonly held belief that runs counter to heavenly wisdom. In what ways does this "common wisdom" shape peoples' choices and reactions? In what ways does it lead to fragmentation and division?

2. Our responses and actions either confirm or contradict the message of the gospel. Can you think of a person or situation in which the gospel was undermined because of how someone responded to challenge? How might nonbelievers perceive the gospel if Christians are driven by fleshly passions?

3. Think of someone in your community who embodies heavenly wisdom. Describe how this person acts and relates to others. How do their actions and choices stand in contrast to those around them? How do they bring peace to conflicts?

4. If you lead a community of Christians, whether online or in person, how do you handle disagreements between members? In what ways do you see the group leaning into earthly wisdom instead of heavenly wisdom? Do members have the freedom and vulnerability to speak into one another's conduct if it is out of step with the gospel?

Looking Ahead

Given our current environment, it's hard to imagine how we can move forward together. But James promises that heavenly wisdom is "pure, then peace-loving, gentle, compliant, full of mercy and good fruits, unwavering, and without pretense. And the fruit of righteousness is sown in peace by those who cultivate peace" (3:17–18). Heavenly wisdom promises a harvest of healing and restoration that will one day be fully realized when Jesus himself reigns over all things.

1. Read Colossians 1:15–20. The apostle Paul writes that the goal of Christ's death is "to reconcile everything to himself . . . by making peace through his blood, shed on the cross" (v. 20). How does this change your understanding of the gospel and the return of Christ?

2. To what degree do you think God is calling Christians to embody heavenly wisdom in their communities right now? In what way might he be calling you to tame the fire and "cultivate peace"? How would this look forward to Christ's coming rule?

3. What role do you think confession and repentance play in our pursuit of heavenly wisdom? What would it look like to commit our present challenges to prayer, praying "Thy kingdom come"?

4. What do you hope to personally gain from this study? How do you hope to be equipped to recognize and pursue wisdom and live a life that testifies to the coming peace of Christ?

Prayer of Confession and Commitment

Father, I confess that I am often driven by earthly wisdom and react out of my sinful desires. I need you to teach me true wisdom. Please give me a heart wholly devoted and submitted to your ways. Make my life a witness to the wisdom and goodness of Jesus Christ. In his name, Amen.

Chapter 2

POOR IN SPIRIT AND IN THE RIGHT KINGDOM

Rebecca McLaughlin

"Blessed are the poor in spirit, for the
kingdom of heaven is theirs."
—Matthew 5:3

On May 19, 2018, the eyes of the world were fixed on the town where I was born. Windsor is home to the Queen. In 2018, it hosted the wedding of Prince Harry and American actress Meghan Markle. As I watched the wedding on TV, I felt nostalgic. My brother sang in the choir of St. George's Chapel, where Harry and Meghan tied the knot. As they drove through Windsor in their horse-drawn carriage, I recognized the streets I paced as a kid. But despite all my connections to the place, I hadn't been invited to the wedding.

Shocking, right?

Why was I left out of this event in my hometown? Was it because I'm not related to the Queen? Or because I don't personally know either Meghan or Harry? Or because I'm not a celebrity? It was all these things combined! At the end of the day, I'm not posh enough, or rich enough, or famous enough to get an invite to a royal wedding. I'm guessing you're not either!

If we look back over our lives, I'm sure we've all had plenty of experience of *not* making the cut. That friend group we aren't cool enough to join. That job we didn't get. That guy we longed to date.

That neighborhood we can't afford. Perhaps even at church we feel like an outsider—hanging out on the fringes, not really part of the crew. At a Christian conference a few years ago, I found myself sobbing in my room because I'd been left out by other women. That feeling of exclusion really stings.

One of the things I love about Jesus is that he gets it. He was rejected by his spiritual community, abandoned by his closest friends, and driven out of his hometown. He faced poverty and mockery, hunger and thirst. And when he taught about *his* kingdom, he said that feeling like you're not good enough to enter is the very thing you need to get in. In fact, unlike the top-down invite list to a royal wedding, he invites people to his kingdom from the bottom up.

Who Is Really Blessed?

If you're on social media, I'm sure you've seen a post with "#blessed." People pair this hashtag with perfect pictures of their spouse, their kids, their house, or their vacation. We're #blessed when everything is great. That's what we post about online: shiny, happy pictures, not footage of us crying on the floor. But when Jesus preached his famous Sermon on the Mount, he must have missed the memo. Instead of saying, "Blessed are the happy, healthy, wealthy, and popular," he said, "Blessed are the poor in spirit, for the kingdom of heaven is theirs" (Matt. 5:3).

This is the first of Jesus' upside-down blessings that we'll look at in this book. Trust me, you won't find it printed on a mug! Who wants to be poor in spirit—worn down, broken, needy, low—when you could be #blessed? Who wants to be humbled when you could be proud? Who wants to be crying on the kitchen floor when you could be lying on a tropical beach, taking some "me time" away from your perfect life? Life coaches tell us, "You are enough!" But Jesus picks the folks who aren't. He says the "poor in spirit" are *truly* blessed, because the kingdom of heaven is theirs.

So, what is this kingdom like?

Jesus' Topsy-Turvy Kingdom

If you read the Gospel accounts of Jesus' life, you'll find he talks a lot about God's kingdom. In fact, one of Jesus' titles is *Christ*, which means God's promised King. *Jesus Christ* means *King Jesus*! But Jesus' kingdom is a topsy-turvy place. In his first sermon in his hometown—the one that got him thrown out—Jesus said he had come to bring good news to the poor, release to prisoners, recovery of sight to the blind, and freedom to the oppressed (Luke 4:18–20). In his kingdom, the seemingly *least* important people are the most important.

Jesus' upside-down view of power is hard for us to grasp. It was hard for his first followers too. One day, two of Jesus' disciples came to him and asked if they could sit on his left and right hand in his glory. Jesus replied that they had no idea what they were asking for. He explained that in his kingdom, "whoever wants to become great among you will be your servant, and whoever wants to be first among you will be a slave to all. For even the Son of Man" [that's Jesus himself] "did not come to be served, but to serve, and to give his life as a ransom for many" (Mark 10:43–45).

You see, Jesus was God's promised freedom-bringing, death-defying, everlasting King. But he wasn't going to kick the Romans out and restore Israel to some picture-perfect moment in the past, as many of his fellow Jews had hoped. He was going to die a shameful, agonizing death on a Roman cross to ransom many people out of slavery to sin. Jesus is the greatest hero the world has ever seen. But he won his greatest victory by looking like a total failure.

So, who does King Jesus invite into his kingdom? Failures. Rejects. Poor people. Prostitutes. Criminals. Anyone from anywhere who realizes they *aren't* good enough for God. Jesus was crucified between two criminals. One of them shouted, "Aren't you supposed to be the King? Save yourself and us as well!" But the other one admitted he was getting what he deserved for his crimes, and he said, "Jesus, remember me when you come into your kingdom." Jesus replied, "Truly, I tell you, today you will be with me in paradise" (Luke 23:43).

In Jesus' kingdom, the ticket in is knowing quite how much we need him. We need to be poor in spirit to realize we need a Savior who can make us right with God. And *anyone* from *anywhere* who comes to Jesus like that gets in.

If your life isn't turning out the way you'd hoped, he'll take you. If your honest image isn't #blessed, he'll take you. If your marriage is on the rocks, he'll take you. If you're divorced or in a bad relationship, he'll take you. If you're single and feeling like you don't fit in at church, he'll take you. If you've lost your job, he'll take you. If you're lonely or depressed or struggling in your faith, Jesus is here with his arms open wide. In *his* kingdom, you'll fit right in. "Blessed are the poor in spirit," says Jesus, "for the kingdom of heaven is theirs."

The Struggle

If being poor in spirit is the hallmark of those who enter Jesus' kingdom, what's the opposite? It's thinking we are #blessed apart from Christ. It's seeing Jesus as the optional cosmetic surgery to our lives, not the heart transplant we'll die without. In other words, it's pride. Pride takes many forms, as we'll see in this book. But since this chapter's blessing centers on God's *kingdom* (and because the remaining Beatitudes tell us how citizens of that kingdom should carry themselves and engage with others), let's look at a particular kind of pride that can get in the way of our spiritual citizenship: pride in our earthly kingdom or nation.

What do I mean? Well, many of us agree with all that the Bible says about Jesus' "anyone from anywhere" kingdom—in theory. But in practice, there's a struggle. Jesus' kingdom isn't bound by borders, but we are. Our perspective is limited to the country in which we live. It may be easy to tell the difference between Christ's heavenly kingdom and an earthly one when we really think about it, at the head level. But it's harder to distinguish at the heart level. Growing up in England, I learned songs that made it sound like Britain had a special relationship with God. In any conflicts Britain had with other nations,

God was definitely on our side, and because Britain was historically "a Christian country," I tended to see British history through that lens. I remember learning a song claiming Britain's special status as being blessed by God that imagined guardian angels singing, "Rule Britannia, Britannia rules the waves. Britons never, never, never will be slaves!"

My husband grew up in Oklahoma with a similar sense of national pride. Whatever land we live in—Britain, America, or otherwise—if our country has been influenced by Christianity in some way, we can start seeing our nation as "God's country," as if God has some sort of unique relationship with our people compared to other people groups across the world, or even other people within our country who have a different racial or national heritage from us. This mistaken thinking can gradually fill us up with a proud spirit that trusts in our country as God's favorite, which works against us being poor in spirit and against us seeing Jesus' actual kingdom at work.

Now, there's nothing wrong with loving one's earthly country. Despite having lived in America for thirteen years, I still love my homeland! But if we're followers of Jesus, we can't get trapped in the snare of national pride (which moves from love-of-country to idolatry-of-country), assuming our land has a special relationship with God that sets it apart from other nations. This thinking can't be right because God's kingdom—his "territory," or "realm," or "country"—belongs to people who are poor in spirit from *anywhere* and *everywhere*. It started in the Middle East and quickly spread around the world. And once we enter Jesus' kingdom, we need to start taking on his kingdom's values, and we'll find they're out of joint with the values around us—even the values we might sometimes see in church.

King of All Nations

Prince Harry's marriage to Meghan Markle brought love across racial and cultural difference into the royal family. Harry is white. Meghan is black. Harry is British. Meghan is American. A couple of generations ago, their marriage would have been unthinkable, and sadly, their interview with Oprah in March 2021 revealed that even today, Meghan's racial heritage made life extremely hard for her as she entered the royal family. This exposes the ugly stain of racism in my own country, a stain that still persists today and is utterly at odds with the claim that Britain is a "Christian country." Because in Jesus' kingdom, love across racial and cultural and national difference has been part of the deal from the first. We tend to miss this, because the racial and national barriers of Jesus' day are different from our own.

In Jesus' famous Parable of the Good Samaritan, a man is robbed and left for dead by the side of the road (Luke 10:25–37). Two Jewish religious leaders walk past and avoid the man. But then a Samaritan comes by, draws near, and cares for him. Jesus' original audience would have been shocked by this story. Samaritans were the Jew's most hated ethnic enemies, and here was Jesus telling a story in which a Samaritan was the moral *hero*! Jesus told this story to explain the heart of the Bible's moral teaching: the command to love your neighbor as yourself (Luke 10:27–29). Loving your neighbor, Jesus explained, means showing love across racial and national difference. It means loving people you were raised to hate.

Jesus didn't just preach about love across racial and national difference. He lived it. For example, in John's Gospel, the longest private conversation Jesus has with anyone is with a Samaritan woman (John 4:1–26). In those days, it would have been weird for a Jewish teacher to talk alone with a woman. It would have been super weird to talk to a *Samaritan* woman. Jews avoided Samaritans like the plague. What's more, this woman had five husbands and was now living with a man she wasn't married to. In the terms of Jewish culture, she was about as bad as a woman could get. She was shocked that Jesus was even talking to her! But he chose her for his kingdom when others thought she was ethnic and moral trash.

After his resurrection, Jesus told his disciples that he was rightful King of all the earth, so they should go and make disciples of *all* nations (Matt. 28:18–19). On the day of Pentecost—the birthday of the church—a crowd including people from modern-day Iran, Iraq, Turkey, Egypt, and Libya heard the message about Jesus, and three thousand people were baptized (Acts 2:5–41). People sometimes think of Christianity as being originally white. But it wasn't. On Day One, brown-skinned apostles preached about a brown-skinned Savior to a multiethnic crowd. Later in Acts, we meet the first known individual black Christian, when Philip is sent to witness to an Ethiopian man (Acts 8:26–40). And as the New Testament unfolds, we see people from all sorts of different national and ethnic backgrounds coming together as believers. Not "separate but equal," as segregation laws in America once ruled, but one body together in Christ (1 Cor. 12:12–27).

Finally, in the last book of the Bible, we see a vision of God's kingdom including "a great multitude that no one could number, from every nation, from all tribes and peoples and languages, standing before the throne and before the Lamb, clothed in white robes, with palm branches in their hands" (Rev. 7:9 ESV). Jesus is the King not of one people and nation, but of a massive multitude of people from *every* tribe, and language, and nation. He'll take the poor in spirit, the losers, the rejects, the spiritual failures from anywhere and everywhere. We only have to put our trust in him.

When you think about it, it's lucky for you and me that Jesus' kingdom doesn't depend on our racial or national heritage. After all, Jesus was a brown-skinned, Middle-Eastern Jew. I don't know what your racial or national background is. But chances are, you're not a Middle-Eastern Jew. As a white European myself, my very salvation depends on the fact that Jesus loved people from ethnic backgrounds different from his own. Thank the Lord that we don't have to hail from his hometown or his country, nor do we have to look like him, to be a citizen of his kingdom!

So, what does Jesus' kingdom look like now?

Discerning Jesus' Kingdom

If you've got a mug in your hand right now, lift it up and look at the bottom. The mug I'm holding says, "Kent Pottery, 1887." I'm guessing your mug says something about the company that made it too. You see, centuries ago, manufacturers of fine China started putting "crown marks" on the bottoms of their mugs to prove they were authentic. Mug makers still do that today. It's like that with Jesus' kingdom: to see if it's authentic, you have to look at it from the bottom up.

In fact, in Jesus' famous Parable of the Sheep and the Goats, he described a day in the future when he would come back to the earth as King, "sit on his glorious throne," and judge people by how they treated the poor and sick, the prisoners and the immigrants, the naked and the destitute (Matt. 25:31–46). Loving people the world perceives to be at the bottom of the pile is what citizens of Jesus' kingdom do.

As I've learned more about Jesus' *anyone* from *anywhere, bottom-up* approach to his own kingdom, I've had to let go of the idea that my country has some kind of exceptional relationship with God that makes it superior to other nations. I've had to untangle the kingdom of heaven—whose citizens come from all different nations—from the kingdom of Great Britain. Yes, my nation has been influenced by Christianity in various places and at various times, and it includes those who are citizens of heaven, but the two aren't the same. In fact, if I take Jesus' multinational, multiethnic, bottom-up approach seriously, I can't help but recognize that the history of racism and white supremacy in my country is totally against Jesus' kingdom.

See, it's easy for us today to look back longingly to a time when Britain and America were Christian countries. If we wind the clock back, we'll find there was a time when the vast majority of people identified as Christians, when prayers were prayed in public schools, when marriage between one man and one woman was the only legal option, and when abortion was illegal. But at the time when all this was true in my country, poor people in Britain were often terribly exploited and Britain was colonizing other countries and placing them under imperial rule. What's more, while British people were singing, "Britons never, never, never will be slaves," British slave traders were enslaving millions of Africans, cramming them onto slave ships where many died, and selling those who survived to white people in America. Their labor was exploited, their bodies were abused, and whatever sense of family they were able to build up was routinely torn apart as children were sold away from their parents and husbands away from their wives.

When slavery was finally abolished in America in 1865, Jim Crow laws were almost immediately put in place. For nearly a hundred years—right up to 1965—these laws made sure that black Americans did not enjoy equality with whites. Thousands were wrongly imprisoned and forced back into unpaid labor. Thousands were beaten or lynched by white mobs. Segregation made sure black people weren't able to access the same jobs, schools, bathrooms, or bus seats as whites, and while black Americans were legally *allowed* to vote, most were stopped from *actually* voting. When black people protested this kind of injustice, they risked being fired, imprisoned, or worse. For example, in 1963, a poor black woman from Mississippi named Fannie Lou Hamer found herself in prison for sitting in a white-only section in a bus terminal. She was beaten so badly that one of her kidneys was permanently damaged and she nearly lost the vision in one eye. This is just one of thousands of examples of the terrible injustice toward black people that has plagued American history—as well as injustice toward Native Americans, Chinese Americans, and Latina/o Americans. When we look from the bottom up, we don't see the crown mark of King Jesus on any of this.

You may be wondering, why dredge all of this up? Because, like I said before, it can be easy for us to mix up the kingdoms. It's easy to assume we're living in God's country, in his kingdom, simply because our nation has been affected by Christian values in certain places and times, while remaining blind to the places where, in those very same periods of time, Christian values were not upheld at all.

For example, many Christians look back at the 1960s as the moment when things started to go wrong. At that time, the sexual revolution was celebrating sex outside of marriage and questioning religious norms. A movement was growing to make abortion legal in all states, resulting in the famous *Roe v. Wade* ruling of 1973. We are right to be distressed by this. In Jesus' topsy-turvy kingdom, unborn babies matter desperately, and any form of sex outside male-female marriage is clearly prohibited for Christians—not because God doesn't like us having fun, but because this incredibly intimate and vulnerable act is a picture of Jesus' love for his church and should always be backed up by loving, lifelong commitment. But the 1960s was also the time when the Civil Rights Movement was finally getting some measure of justice for black Americans. So, when we look back to the time before the '60s as the good old days when America was a Christian country, we act like the suffering of black brothers and sisters doesn't matter. According to Jesus, it matters very much.

Just like it can be hard for us to face the bad things in our family history—especially if we come from a Christian family—it can be really hard to face the ways in which the country we love *hasn't* upheld Christian values. But if we're followers of Jesus, we don't need to put our hope in our national pride. No earthly kingdom or country can be the kingdom of heaven for us. In fact, if we listen to Jesus, putting all our pride and hope in our country stops us from entering his kingdom, because the kingdom of heaven doesn't belong to people who are proud but to the poor in spirit.

So, what hope is there for us today?

What Hope Is There Today?

Many Christians today fear a future in which Christians might lose their jobs or even go to prison for standing for traditional Christian views of sex and marriage. Many fear that immigration has eroded American's Christian identity. But I think we have a much more hopeful story to tell—a story in which Jesus' topsy-turvy kingdom in America isn't shrinking, but actually growing.

How so, you might wonder? Starting in the 1700s thousands of enslaved black people in America were putting their trust in Christ. As they heard the message of Jesus, they realized he was on their side. Some were encouraged by their white slaveholders. Others were persecuted for their faith: stopped from reading the Bible, beaten for attending services, forced to gather underground to worship the King. They knew Jesus understood their suffering, because he had died on a cross for their sake. How sweet to their ears must Jesus' words have been: "Blessed are the poor in spirit, for the kingdom of heaven is theirs!"

This river of faith ran down through generations of black Americans. The leading abolitionists were spurred on by their faith in Christ, and when the Civil Rights Movement came, it was at heart a Christian movement. The Rev. Dr. Martin Luther King Jr. preached from the Bible and called America to be what it was meant to be: a nation built on the biblical belief that all human beings are created equal. Today, black Americans are the *most* likely people in America to identify as Christians, to attend church weekly, to read their Bibles, and to pray. Meanwhile, rather than eroding America's Christian heritage, immigration is bringing in a wealth of evangelical Christians from across the world. In the city next to mine, English is the third most commonly spoken language at evangelical churches, after Portuguese and Creole, and the building where my church meets also hosts congregations of believers from Haiti and Nepal!

Of course, not all immigrants are Christians. White Europeans like me are some of the *least* likely to be followers of Jesus. But many immigrants from Latin America and Africa have come here with their hope in Christ. Increasing racial diversity in America doesn't spell the end of America's Christian heritage. It brings more workers to the harvest field, as Christians from all racial backgrounds testify together to the saving power of Christ! To be sure, fewer people in America today will *say* they're Christians than during the time of slavery or segregation. But it may be that more people are *actually* Christians today—not just fitting in with the culture around them, but following the topsy-turvy, freedom-bringing King.

In 1963, Fannie Lou Hamer had lain beaten and abused in a prison cell. But by 1964, she'd become such an important leader in the Civil Rights Movement that President Lyndon Johnson sent his right-hand man to ask her what she *really* wanted. She's reported to have answered, "What I really want is the immediate establishment of God's kingdom here on earth." We won't see Jesus' topsy-turvy, multiracial, freedom-bringing, everlasting kingdom fully established here on the earth until he comes again. But here today, instead of putting all our pride and hope in places like Britain or America to be the kingdom of God for us, let's live as subjects of Christ's *true* kingdom, poor in spirit toward our King and rich in love toward those he came to save. Instead of looking up longingly to palaces like Windsor Castle—wishing we were important enough to get a royal invitation—let's look down lovingly to find the people Jesus calls us to serve. "Blessed are the poor in spirit," Jesus declared, "for the kingdom of heaven is theirs" (Matt. 5:3).

Application

Looking In

Sometimes it's hard to know if we're being poor in spirit, or if we're living for the right kingdom. Use these questions to help you as you examine your own life and heart:

1. The way of the world is to be proud in spirit. Why do you think that feels so natural to you sometimes?

2. In your Christian journey, when can you remember being poor in spirit? How did Jesus meet you in that place? What things typically tempt you away from maintaining that posture, toward the posture of pride, and has it ever been pride in your country?

3. What earthly kingdom or nation do you live in (America, Britain, Mexico, Nigeria, etc.), and in what ways has the past of that country failed to be the kingdom of God or express its values? In what ways have you put too much trust or pride in that nation, and why do you think you do this sometimes?

4. How does it feel to let go of that and turn your eyes to Jesus' topsy-turvy, international, multiethnic kingdom instead?

Looking Up

When we examine ourselves, we are forced to face the ways we fall short of Jesus' teaching—and that can sting sometimes. Let's look up together, to our Lord whose arms are open to anyone who has failed, and who helps us change.

1. Jesus welcomes "anyone from anywhere" who will come to him with humble, needy, broken hearts. How are you tempted to get stuck in guilt and condemnation when you're challenged by God's Word, instead of approaching Jesus with the belief that he will take you in?

2. In what ways has God used this chapter to convict your heart? How does Jesus' work on the cross speak to any failure you sense before the Lord?

3. Jesus wants you in his kingdom and he has a role for you to play. In what ways do you struggle to believe that?

Looking Out

Zooming out from our individual experience, let's consider the way Jesus' teaching impacts the way we carry ourselves within our broader culture.

1. In what ways do you see our culture prioritize being proud in spirit instead of poor in spirit? In what ways have you seen our society put all its hope in the wrong kingdom?

2. When you go to church, how do you act toward people who show up for the first time, or whose lives look like they're in a mess? Rather than avoiding them or leaving them on the fringes, what could you do to be more like Christ who draws near, welcomes, and includes people?

3. How can you pray for and encourage the people in your life who worry that Christianity is under threat and feel hopeless or defensive?

4. What opportunities do you see to build relationships and work together with Christians who are different from you in terms of race or culture? What opportunities do you see to help those you lead do the same?

Looking Ahead

Zooming out even more, let's think through how Jesus' teaching helps us prepare for the day when he will come to make all things new.

1. We aren't going to see the full establishment of the kingdom of God on earth until Jesus returns, but we can be part of building it here and now as we go forward toward that day. How can you help mobilize people at your church to be part of that?

2. How does the future vision of "every nation, tribe, people, and language" gathered around Jesus' throne change the way you handle your ordinary life and schedule today?

Prayer of Confession and Commitment

Father, I confess that instead of being poor in spirit before you, and serving those the world considers lowly, I have lived in proud ways, putting my ultimate hope in the wrong places and avoiding some of the people you came to save! Forgive me for mixing up your heavenly kingdom with any kingdom or nation of the earth, and help me put my hope not in my nation, but in you, the King over every tribe and tongue and nation. Change me into a person who loves anyone from anywhere, just like you. In Jesus' name, amen. ♨

Chapter 3

MOURNING SIN IN A WORLD THAT FORGETS IT

Elizabeth Woodson

> *"Blessed are those who mourn, for*
> *they will be comforted."*
> —Matthew 5:4

> *Each one of us has lived through some devastation,*
> *some loneliness, some weather superstorm or*
> *spiritual superstorm; when we look at each other*
> *we must say, I understand. I understand how*
> *you feel because I have been there myself.*[1]
> —Maya Angelou

There are few conversations I remember as distinctly as this one. Even though it feels like it happened yesterday, it took place years ago. I was in my pastor's office, participating in a conflict-resolution conversation, and I was the offending party.

Erykah[2] was a volunteer on a team I led during my early years in church ministry. I will admit, those years were not my finest moments. I was learning how to lead as a recovering people-pleaser. So, my

---

[1] Maya Angelou, *Rainbow in the Cloud* (New York: Random House, 2014), Kindle Edition, 27.

[2] While this story is true, the name and some identifying details have been changed to protect the privacy of the person involved.

attempts to handle conflict were clunky, messy, and unnecessarily complicated.

To say that we didn't get along would be an understatement. Our relationship had been positive at the beginning, but it deteriorated quickly. After months of hard conversations and awkward interactions, Erykah eventually left the ministry. It wasn't until a few years later, as we were sitting in that pastor's office, that I would learn the extent to which my leadership, or lack thereof, had wounded her.

Prompted by our pastor to explain her perspective, Erykah shared how I had not been kind, clear, and gracious to her in the way that I led. She recounted in-person conversations and emails that had left her feeling unloved and unwanted. Now, I'll be honest, I could have defended myself in some places where I didn't agree with her or where I didn't think she was telling the full story. But here's the thing: some of what she said was painfully true. As Erykah continued to talk about her experience of me, I became more and more convicted about my behavior. I realized that in trying to deal with the ways I believed she had sinned against me, I had sinned against Erykah.

The Wisdom of Mourning

In Matthew 5:4, Jesus continues to unpack the character that his followers should embody. After telling them that the blessed life is found in an awareness of their spiritual poverty, he tells them this same blessing is also given to those who mourn.

If you are anything like me, you have one major question after reading this verse—*what should we be mourning?*

Mourning Sin

While it might seem like an odd connection, this process of feeling or expressing deep sorrow is the natural outflow of the previous beatitude.[3] A recognition of our spiritual poverty should immediately lead us into a place of emotional brokenness. We become overwhelmed by the reality of our sinfulness, its eternal consequences, and our inability to be righteous outside of Christ.

During the Sermon on the Mount, Jesus is speaking to an audience of Jewish men and women. So as they thought about their spiritual poverty, they would immediately remember not only their sin but the historic sins of their people—the nation of Israel.

In the beginning pages of Scripture, God initiates a covenantal relationship with Israel. He makes an agreement with them, showing them how to love him and love one another. But as we've all seen in our reading of the Bible, Israel has a hard time holding up their end of the agreement. Instead of obeying God, they persist in a life of sin. Specifically, God continually calls out Israel for their sins of idolatry, injustice, and greed (Isa. 2:8; Hos. 4:12).

Now, the sins of Israel were both individual and corporate. In their individual lives, people were making daily, personal decisions to disobey God. On top of that, they sometimes sinned *together* as a people, creating various ungodly systems by which their society would function. This does not mean that every system they created was wrong, but rather, because of sin, some of them were. When we read the words of the prophets, in particular Amos, we can see this pattern of corporate sin. In Amos 2, we read about how Israel withheld justice from the vulnerable and sold other humans for economic gain. But, an ungodly system, rooted in greed, would have been required for these sinful atrocities to take place.

And we can all see the irony, can't we? Israel was intimately acquainted with the suffering these sins caused. For four hundred years, Israel had languished in slavery, living under the oppressive rule of Egypt. They knew what it was to be the recipient of unjust treatment that was motivated by greed. From this deep place of suffering, they called out to God for deliverance, and he answered their prayers.

---

[3] https://www.merriam-webster.com/dictionary/mourn

Yet somehow, generations later, they ended up operating in many of the same unjust and sinful behaviors.

When Jesus tells Jews, "blessed are those who mourn . . ." this history is a large part of what they would mourn. They would mourn how their individual and collective sins brought about grievous consequences, for, under their watch, people were mistreated, oppressed, and even killed. They would remember how generations of sinful behavior resulted in them being in exile for seventy years. But most of all, they would remember how their sin dishonored God, the One who created them, delivered them out of slavery, and committed to faithfully love them.

A slow and arduous process, mourning requires both *remembrance* and *repentance*. While reflecting on their past sin, Israel would respond by personally and corporately repenting for how they had broken the covenant they made with God. Through an emotional and sacred process, Israel would take responsibility for their sins, whether individual or corporate (Dan. 9:1–19; Neh. 1:4–7).

They would also mourn the suffering they experienced because of the sins of *other* people, both past and present. They would remember how their people had mourned in sackcloth and ashes years before now, crying out to God for deliverance, provision, and justice (Esther 4:1). And they would also lament the current mistreatment they faced from the Romans. Knowing no other way to resolve their pain, all they could do was seek the help of the only One who could. But Israel's mourning also reflected their deeper longing for the kingdom of God. They longed for a day when sin would be no more. In the same way, when we mourn our sin and the sin of the world, we're also longing for the day when God's kingdom will come in fullness, and sin will no longer be part of our reality.

Met with Comfort

But, if we read Matthew 5:4 too quickly, we can miss the beauty of its second half. In this short phrase, Jesus promises our mourning will be met with comfort, both in the present and the future. Echoing the words of Isaiah 61:1–2, Jesus tells his Jewish audience that this Old Testament promise of comfort has been fulfilled. His sacrifice on the cross would pay the price for the sins of both Israel and the entire world, offering a restored and right relationship with God to anyone who would believe.

There is also a future comfort in Jesus' final work of restoration. Sin has left all of creation broken, which means we still suffer injustice, experiencing the effects of other people's sin. Even though this suffering can be overwhelming, we suffer with hope, because our pain does not go unnoticed by God. In fact, because "the LORD is a just God" and "all his ways are just," he uses his people to reflect and bring about his justice in the world (Isa. 30:18; Deut. 32:4). Yet, alongside this present reality of hope, we also have a future hope in the glorious return of Christ, who one day will restore *all* of creation to perfection (Rev. 22).

Through Christ, the power of sin has been broken; the weight of our grief has been lifted. But this relief and consolation only comes *after* mourning. So the wisdom we seek can only come through a consistent process of remembering and grieving sin.

The problem is, the world doesn't want us to remember sin.

It works hard to make sure we forget.

The Power of Spiritual Forgetfulness

Honestly, working with Erykah had been tough. No matter how hard I tried, she would consistently push back against my leadership and authority. Quickly exhausting my "nice church leader" plan, I went back to what I knew—my "get it done" management skills that I learned while working in the marketplace.

But somehow along the way, I subconsciously decided that the end justified the means. I stopped seeing Erykah as a person to be loved and treated her as a problem to be solved. Quick to cast judgment when we butted heads, I was slow to give compassion and grace. I was very clear in terms of her shortcomings, but was blind to my own. Regrettably, I rationalized or simply ignored my behavior because, in my mind, I wasn't the problem. Erykah was.

While there are many distinguishing characteristics of our current culture, self-examination is not one of them. On social media or a group text thread, news travels fast. But our criticism of someone's actions or character travels even faster. Unconcerned with the substance of our "truth" and the method of its communication, we are quick to call out the behavior or ideas of those we disagree with. The problem is that we often do so from a place of unchecked self-righteousness.

As you probably already know by now, research shows that social media is built on algorithms that typically only show us information that matches our interests or tastes.[4] So, we are more prone to see posts that contain information we agree with, functionally placing us in what many call an online "echo chamber." While providing a source of legitimate community, this ideological isolation can also make us blind. With each post we like and share, we become more proficient at seeing the sin of those with whom we disagree and more inept at seeing our own.

On the other hand, the suffering of the world can be hard to understand, and the internet provides us with an overflow of easy answers. Backed by the seemingly unanimous agreement within our online communities, we can grow to have a false sense of confidence. We don't take the time to make sure our ideas are actually *true*, nor do we critically think about how our beliefs and actions could be harmful to others. Most of all, we never stop to think that we might be a part of the problem we are working so hard to fight. Unintentionally, we can often become the perpetrators of falsehoods that lead to sinful and destructive behavior.

---

[4] Katherine J. Wu, "Radical ideas spread through social media. Are the algorithms to blame?" PBS, March 28, 2019, https://www.pbs.org/wgbh/nova/article/radical-ideas-social-media-algorithms/.

If being blind to our own sin wasn't enough of a struggle, we also live in a culture that has a growing love for sin. Disrespect has become a culturally acceptable pathway to achieve a goal or make a point. We are rewarded with praise-hand-emojis and "likes" when our words are wrathful, slanderous, unrighteously angry, and abusive (Col. 3:8). In essence, we have become comfortable believing that it's okay to dishonor God's created humanity—his very image in the world—in our attempts to honor him.

It has also become culturally acceptable to ignore or excuse others' sinful actions because we agree with their views or ideas. Instead of seeing sin for what it is, a grievous offense against a holy God, we reduce it to excusable character flaws. Somehow along the way, we decided that in the kingdom of God, the end justifies the means.

We Mourn to Remember

Friend, whether we see the action as being big or small, sin is always serious and costly. When we forget this, we can become self-righteous and detached from the mission of God (Matt. 22:36–40; 28:19–20). In this space of spiritual forgetfulness, we will be prone to dehumanize the people he made in his image. No matter how noble and well-intentioned we may believe ourselves to be, when we dishonor image-bearers in our attempt to do the work of God, we also dishonor God.

Yet, spiritual forgetfulness can simultaneously leave us overwhelmed by the suffering of life. Injustice is real, and many of us know people whose lives have been permanently affected by the sins of other people. But looking to the world to provide answers or vengeance for our pain will only leave us engulfed in a cycle of hopelessness and despair.

When the world tells us to forget our sinfulness, Jesus tells us to mourn it.

When the world tells us to find comfort in false truths and illegitimate justice, Jesus tells us to find comfort in him.

Yet, if we are honest, in comparison to the weight of sin and suffering in the world, the truth of Matthew 5:4 sometimes seems insufficient and shallow. While we can appreciate the sentiment of Jesus' words, it can be hard to see how a posture of "mourning" helps give us the wisdom we need to navigate the sin in the world.

The Power of Story

As I listened to Erykah share her story, the Lord gave me the heart to see her in a new way. I always tell young ministry folks, "People are the way they are for a reason. The quicker you learn that reason, the easier time you will have interacting with them." This piece of wisdom is not a silver bullet, but serves as a simple reminder that everyone has a story. Events in this story often connect directly to the encouraging or challenging interactions they have with you. However, in all my conversations with Erykah, I had never learned her story. I had never thought about how the life experiences she might have had led to our less than stellar relationship.

You see, life stories connect us with someone's humanity. Softening our hearts, we can look past our disagreements to see an image-bearer who God loves just as much as he loves us. This softening does not absolve anyone of accountability or the natural consequences of their sin. But I believe Jesus' call to grieve and hope is a call to remember our own stories and the stories of others. As we step into these intimate and often painful narratives, we experience an internal transformation that empowers us to engage the issues of our day in a new way.

To be a people who mourn our sin means that we interact with others through the lens of our own sinfulness. We not only remember the depth of our fallenness but grieve the consequences of our sin. As the recipients of an eternal salvation that was not free, we continually remember the suffering and death of Jesus. Yet, this place of deep sorrow forms something beautiful in us—graciousness. In the words of Paul Tripp, "no one gives grace better than a person who is deeply persuaded that he needs it himself and is being given it in Christ."[5]

Our posture of mourning also leads us to lament how sin has ravaged our world and the lives of all its inhabitants, both past and present. Since I grew up in America, my nation's history comes to mind, as it is full of stories of people who have been treated as less than a human being, as if they did not bear the likeness of God.

But, as it was with Israel and every other country in a fallen world, our broken and checkered past is not only a story of how individuals sinned against one another. It is also a story of how individuals— some of them Christians—worked together to create public policies and institutional practices to perpetuate their sin, whether that be slavery, the Trail of Tears, Jim Crow laws, or abortion. Indeed, our two-hundred-plus years of nationhood is fraught with tragic stories of image-bearers systemically mistreating other image-bearers.

As believers, this is not a history we ignore, minimize, or reject. That is the response of those in earthly kingdoms who cannot remember or face the reality of sin. Instead, as citizens of heaven's kingdom, we show the world what it looks like to acknowledge, grieve, and lament histories like this one, whether in our own society or any other. Even when these stories make us uncomfortable, our love for God and those made in his image should be a stronger motivator for our response than our discomfort.

In addition to graciousness, mourning produces within us a deep well of compassion. Recognizing the weight of sin's collateral damage, we grieve the men, women, children, and unborn souls whose lives have been cut short or traumatized by the sin of our country and this world.

---

[5] Paul Tripp, *Dangerous Calling* (Wheaton, IL: Crossway, 2012), 122.

We Mourn to Love Well

Friend, the issues of our day are not simple. They are very complex. When hard conversations—the ones that immediately divide people—come up, we can become uncomfortable or angry. But, instead of being defensive or dismissive, we should see these conversations as an opportunity to walk in wisdom—graciously and compassionately loving our neighbor well (Matt. 22:36–40; Luke 10:25–37).

When politics or racism or sexuality or abortion or any other "fire starting" issue comes up in conversation, Christians should not have our boxing gloves up, standing ready to fight. Rather, we should have the posture of one who stands ready to mourn, wherever there is evidence of sin or suffering. This does not mean we have to back down from our convictions, but it does mean we listen with an openness to hear how we might be part of the problem and have the willingness to help bear the burdens of another. The Christian in the kingdom of God is one who, when hearing about anything that may have sin involved in it, first takes the posture of a mourner. *This* is how we handle the fiery conversations the world says we cannot have.

Simultaneously, we also choose to be a conduit of God's comfort to humanity. Through Jesus, God fully accomplishes salvation for us, rescuing us from judgment for sin into fellowship with him, and then restores the creation in which we can enjoy our new life together with him forever.[6] To echo the words of Anthony Bradley, "We seek to call God's people to himself through evangelism *and to liberate creation from the power of the devil until Christ returns.*"[7]

Our love for Jesus should compel us to participate in this mission of God as we wait for our future and eternal comfort to come.

---

[6] Trevin Wax, "Gospel Definitions: Tim Keller," March 7, 2008, https://www.thegospelcoalition.org/blogs/trevin-wax/gospel-definitions-tim-keller/.

[7] Anthony Bradley, "Commission Christianity Keeps Blacks Away from Evangelicalism," *Fathom*, March 11, 2019, emphasis added, https://www.fathommag.com/stories/the-great-commission-christianity-keeps-blacks-away-from-evangelicalism.

The Power of Hope

After Erykah finished recounting her experience with me, I responded with sincere words of regret and apology. Soon after, the conversation ended, and Erykah and I went our separate ways. Even though that was the last time we saw each other, it was not the last time I thought about that conversation. I think about it often actually, mostly when I am in a situation of conflict.

The truth is, I don't like to remember. It makes me uncomfortable and can fill me with shame.

Still, this process of remembering my story, her story, and God's story, compels me to be different. I mourn my sin because I want to learn from my sin; I don't repeat it.

Jesus' words to the crowd in Matthew 5:4 were spoken with a deep understanding of the people's plight. He knew their struggles, the oppression they were experiencing under the rule of Rome. Since he is God, he knew their deepest fears, sorrows, and pain. Meeting them in this place of brokenness, Jesus didn't give them super-spiritual answers. He didn't promise that theirs would be a life devoid of difficulty and trouble. Jesus gave them something better—an eternal hope in him.

We Mourn with Hope

Friend, like I've said before, the issues of our day are not simple. They are heavy and complex. The weight of sin and suffering can cause us to check out or to be overwhelmed by despair. Conversely, a blind zeal for God can cause us to sin, becoming detached from his mission as we dehumanize his image-bearers.

The way of wisdom would have us take a different approach. It tells us that the blessed life comes to those who mourn sin. This is the lens through which we view all the difficult issues that have polarized our society. The memory of our sin, and forgiveness through Christ, leads us to respond from a posture of grief, not self-righteousness. We lean into the reality of sin and suffering empowered by his hope. No matter what happens, our comfort is on the way! When Jesus returns, he will make all that is wrong about this world, right.

Imagine what would happen if we actually lived this way.

Imagine a world where all Christians—no matter who they were, what they looked like, or where they were from—were known for being a people of grace, compassion, and hope.

That's the world I want to help build. I pray you do too.

Application

Looking In

To walk in wisdom, we must learn to be honest about our sin. The world, and our flesh, will continuously tempt us to live from a posture of self-righteousness. So, we must be intentional about reflecting on how we have strayed from the ways of Jesus.

1. Why is it important for us to think about and grieve our own sin, the sins of our communities, and the sin going on around us in culture?

2. Think through your recent conversations and social media activity. What sins have you been quick to point out? How are you guilty of practicing those same sins?

3. When you are overwhelmed with the suffering in the world, where do you find comfort? In what ways are you placing your hope in Jesus? In what ways are you placing your hope in the world?

Looking Up

Our process of self-examination does not only involve us. As the Holy Spirit reveals our sin and misplaced hopes, we bring this revelation to God in Christ. In this space of confession and repentance, we reorient ourselves to the truth of the gospel.

1. Read the words of Psalm 139:23–24 to God in prayer. Then, spend a few moments in silence allowing God to examine your heart. Use a journal to write down what he reveals to you. Respond to his revelation with a prayer of confession and repentance.

2. How should Jesus' sacrifice on the cross affect how we view our sin and these sins of others?

3. What can you do to keep the cross of Christ consistently in your purview?

Looking Out

Biblical self-examination gives us the clarity we need to love those around us well, even in the most challenging situations.

1. What current conversations in culture make you the most uncomfortable or upset? Explain why. With whom do you have these conversations?

2. Why is it easy for us to dehumanize those people we disagree with? In what ways have you dehumanized the people you disagree with, in-person and online? Is there anyone you need to ask for forgiveness because of how you treated them?

3. How does an attitude of self-righteousness or spiritual forgetfulness affect our engagement in those discussions? On the flip side, how does an attitude of grace and compassion affect our engagement in those discussions?

4. If you lead other Christians in a group of some sort, would you say your participants regularly mourn their own sin or the sins taking place in our culture? How could you help them develop a healthy lament over sin?

Looking Ahead

As believers it is the hope of comfort in Jesus that gives us vision, empowering us to persist in difficulty and trouble. As we wait for our eternal hope, we push forth the mission of God and work to restore creation from the power of sin and the devil.

1. How should the truth of Matthew 22:36–40 and Matthew 28:19–20 ground us as we seek to navigate the sin and suffering of the world? What does it prevent us from doing? What does it empower us to do? (Read Colossians 3:1–14 and Galatians 5:22–23 to help you with your answer.)

2. The comfort of Jesus includes justice and help for the suffering in the world that he many times enacts through the work of his people (for example, things like the Civil Rights Movement, advocacy for the unborn, and many hospital/orphanage networks are historically tied to the work of Christians). In what ways have you detached issues of justice from the mission of God? Explain why.

3. What impact do you think Christians could have if we sought to lean into the suffering of humanity, people we agree with and those we don't, with an attitude of grace and compassion?

4. What is the future cost of us not doing this? What is the future cost of you not doing this?

Prayer of Confession and Commitment

Lord, I confess that oftentimes, I am quick to see the sins of others before acknowledging my sin. Sometimes, I can even avoid or forget my own sin or the sins of my culture. When I sense conviction over my sin, help me not ignore it or minimize it, but instead, stop and mourn. Help me also to see the suffering of others around me, lamenting with them as they grieve the pain of being sinned against. Use me as an instrument of healing as I reflect your love and your justice in this world. In Jesus' name, amen.

Chapter 4

MEEKNESS IN A WORLD OF PRIDE

Hannah Anderson

"Blessed are the meek, for they will inherit the earth."
—Matthew 5:5 NIV

My fingers flew across the keyboard and my mind whirled. I'd just read an article that detailed the latest political scandal. The corruption was clear, and to me, it was just one more example of how desperately our culture needed gospel correction and the witness of Christians in this moment.

Condensing my thoughts into a string of 280 characters, I paused only briefly before hitting the key that would send them into the ether. Bits of data streamed from my laptop to the router and out of my house. Within milliseconds, my words began showing up on the screens of friends, family, and followers all around the world. And within seconds after that, they were ringing up clicks, likes, and shares. The energy was palpable. "Right on!" "That's so good." "Yes!" "Can I share this?"

Affirmation was fast and furious, confirming not only my perspective on this particular issue but that I was not alone. Like me, other people understood the threat we were facing. Like me, they were concerned about the direction of our culture. And like me, they felt the stress and anxiety of watching unethical people gain power, money, and position. Sure, it was just a post on social media, but in that moment, it felt like so much more. It felt like I was testifying to something important. My words had become a rallying cry. We were joining together in a shared sense of purpose and vision. I sat back in my chair, content.

There was only one problem. Everything I'd just posted was demonstrably and unequivocally untrue.

Wisdom Explained

After calling his followers to learn how to mourn the brokenness of this world, Jesus turns our attention to how cultivating meekness makes us wise: "Blessed are the meek for they will inherit the earth." Meekness is not a word that we commonly use, but it describes the humble serenity that comes from trusting in God and is a theme that runs through the Scripture.[1] In fact, scholars think that Jesus is likely alluding to Psalm 37 where David writes about humbly placing our trust in the Lord when we see evil going unpunished.

Psalm 37 opens with that memorable line "Fret not thyself because of evildoers" (KJV) and explores the angst we feel when the wicked seem to be able to reach their goals but we can't reach ours. For the original audience of Psalm 37, these good goals included dwelling safely in the land of Israel as God had promised them. For those who would hear Jesus' words nearly 1,000 years later, this tension was heightened by living under Roman rule in this very same land.

So when Jesus promises the crowd on the mountainside that the "meek will inherit the earth," he's hitting a particular point of pain for them. But instead of being agitated and worried, they were to "trust in the LORD and do what is good" (Ps. 37:3) and to "commit [their] way to the LORD" (37:5). Live like this, both David and Jesus promise, and God will provide what you're hoping for: "the humble will inherit the land" (Ps. 37:11).

---

[1] Just a few chapters later in Matthew 11, Jesus connects the ideas of meekness, humility, and serenity when he says, "Come unto me all ye that labor and are heavy laden and I will give you rest. Take my yoke upon you, and learn of me; for I *am meek and lowly [humble]* in heart" (Matt. 11:28–29 KJV).

The problem, of course, is that everything in us and everything around us tells us a different story.

Spend any amount of time reading history or even today's headlines and you'll know that the meek do not rule over the earth; the fittest do. The humble do not gain power; earthly wisdom tells us the aggressive do—those who reach up and claim it for themselves. Calm, controlled people will not enjoy security; only those who fight and scrape and clamber and climb to get to the top will. So if you have any hope of surviving this life, you're going to have to learn to fight and protect your own. Meekness is the luxury of the detached and ineffective. You, on the other hand, must never give up. Never give in. Never back down.

The Struggle of Pride

Within a few minutes of posting my ill-conceived commentary, a brave soul noted that perhaps I had misunderstood the article. Then another person said the same. *Was it really as simple as I was making it out to be?* And just like that, my hot take proved to be a mis-take. As more comments began to challenge my opinion, I felt trapped. No one was attacking me personally, but it was clear that I'd written myself into a corner. My heart started racing, my adrenaline pumped, and I assumed a fighting position.

On one hand, I knew that the pushback was valid or at the very least, there were more facts that I needed to consider. On the other, I also knew that my concerns about the larger question were justified—even if I'd gotten the specifics wrong. My goal was good, I reasoned. It was important to get the broader message out and warn people about the danger. I was on the right side of this issue. And because I was, what did it matter that I'd gotten one or two small details incorrect? Folks were simply being picky.

I quickly started thinking of ways I could spin their objections. I could deflect by pointing a finger at the other side. I could nuance my original comment to such a degree as to protect it from criticism. And if all else failed, I could always simply double-down, dig in my heels, and refuse to budge. Who needs to inherit the earth if you can simply hold your ground?

In his book *The Improvement of the Mind*, hymn writer Isaac Watts[2] describes my temptation this way:

> Having asserted his former opinions in a most confident manner, he is tempted now to wink a little against the truth, or prevaricate . . . lest, by admitting conviction, he should . . . [confess] his former folly and mistake; and he has not humility enough for that.[3]

With painful clarity, Watts diagnoses the root of my struggle, one we've touched on before in this book and will probably touch on again: pride. I could not admit I was wrong because I had placed my confidence in myself—in my own ability to understand, my own ability to research, my own ability to know. I had placed confidence in my own ability to fight back the evil I saw.

And just like that, you begin to understand why Jesus calls us to meekness, why wise people must be humble people.

Meekness is not passivity or a lack of fight. It is active trust in the only One who is trustworthy. Meek people don't strive to accomplish even good things in human strength because they don't trust in themselves in the first place. They don't trust in their own intelligence, understanding, power, goodness, or will. They don't fret and exhaust

---

[2] Isaac Watts is the hymn writer behind such well-loved hymns as "When I Survey the Wondrous Cross," "Alas and Did My Savior Bleed," and "Joy to the World!"

[3] Isaac Watts, *The Improvement of the Mind: Or, A Supplement to the Art of Logic: Containing a Variety of Remarks and Rules for the Attainment and Communication of Useful Knowledge in Religion, in the Sciences, and in Common Life; to Which Is Added, a Discourse on the Education of Children and Youth* (Morgan, PA: Soli Deo Gloria Publications, 1998), 13.

themselves in fighting and grasping because they know human frailty and choose instead to put their trust in God.

The proud, however, trust themselves. They trust in human means and human leaders. They "take pride in chariots" as Psalm 20:7 says and put their confidence in men instead of in God (Ps. 118:8). But because they trust in their weapons and leaders to keep them safe, they must forever defend and protect them even when they prove themselves to be faithless and unworthy of trust.

Worse still, because the proud put their trust in human effort, they inevitably turn to all kinds of evil to achieve their goals (as we see in Psalm 37). After all, when you're convinced that the outcome depends on *you*, you'll do anything to reach it. When winning becomes the only thing that matters, you can justify any kind of behavior, language, or deception to do so.

Ultimately the question of meekness is not whether our goal itself is good or bad, but how we are trying to achieve it. *What are willing to do to make sure it happens? Are we depending on ourselves and our human wisdom? Or are we depending on God and his ways?*

Meekness Testifies to the Gospel

Within an hour, someone with training and firsthand knowledge entered the conversation. She kindly began to show me (and the watching world) where my assessment had gone wrong. She provided demonstrable proof that I didn't know what I was talking about, and in God's grace, offered me an opportunity to become wiser. If only I would take it.

I'd like to tell you that I quickly and easily did, but I can't. I knew enough to stop fighting and to stop digging myself deeper, but the battle between meekness and pride was raging inside of me and the only thing I could do at that point was close my laptop and step away. I spent the rest of the afternoon wrestling with the Holy Spirit. I knew I had to return and sort through the conversation, but *did I really have to confess my fault? Did I really have to say "I was wrong?" What if we just chalked it up to difference of opinion and "agreed to disagree"?*

The danger of pride is not simply that we depend on ourselves, but that in depending on ourselves, we limit our ability to grow and benefit from those God places in our lives. Pride limits our ability to become wise because those who believe they don't have anything to learn, won't. Those who fight and strive for power over others will spend their lives maintaining it. And those who can't admit when they are wrong will be doomed to a life of perpetual performance, unable to ever be vulnerable or truly known by others.

This is a particular dilemma for those of us who have been taught that the weight of our Christian witness rests on our performance. If we believe that the success of the gospel depends on us, it is almost impossible to admit mistakes because doing so would detract from our credibility. But what if gospel credibility doesn't come from *our* being right? What if the gospel is proven true, not by our success, but by what happens when we fail?

Meekness frees us from the burden of protecting our "right-ness" because at its core, meekness confesses that the gospel never depended on *us* in the first place. And in this counterintuitive, countercultural way, meekness affirms the gospel even when—especially when—we make a mistake. Instead of performance, meekness calls us to embody the truth through repentance and dependence on God. It calls us to quickly and fully confess our faults and point to the One who never fails.

It calls us to testify to a better way.

Blessed Are the Meek

After a few hours, I was finally able to return to my keyboard. My fingers moved much more slowly this time and I didn't feel the rush of certainty I'd felt earlier in the day. But I also didn't feel shame. And astonishingly, amazingly, as I wrote, the words came easily:

"I'm sorry."

"I was wrong."

"I didn't know what I was talking about."

"Thank you for explaining."

By the time I was done I felt freedom. I felt peace. I also felt connection and gratitude to those who only hours before had felt like a threat.

In the simplest terms I can think of, meekness looks like a person at peace in the midst of challenge and conflict. It is not a person who is detached or uninterested, but a person who trusts in the Lord even in the most difficult times. Even when her own actions bring those difficult times upon her. And because she is at peace, she can respond to others from a place of stability instead of reaction. She can receive correction and even correct herself. She can become wise.

But meekness also guides us when the difficulty comes from outside us too—when we take a stand for an uncomfortable truth or unpopular opinion and face the wrath of the crowd. In these moments, meekness reminds us that we do not endure persecution through our own strength, power, or intelligence. We endure by trusting in God. Listen again to how Psalm 37 describes the way of the meek, those who trust in the Lord instead of in human strength:

> Trust in the LORD . . .
>
> Take delight in the Lord . . .
>
> Commit your way to the Lord . . .
>
> Be silent before the Lord and wait . . .
>
> Do not be agitated . . .
>
> Refrain from anger and give up your rage . . .

So that when we rest patiently in the midst of hard struggles, we witness to a God who will carry us through them. When we refuse to respond to aggression with aggression, we show that we are not trusting in our own strength. When we don't fight to have the last word, we confess that our hope is in someone Greater than our words. And when we acknowledge our faults, we testify that it never depended on us in the first place.

As Christians, we should be the first people to walk in meekness and humility. We should be the first to understand human weakness, the propensity to err, and to think too highly of ourselves. We should also be the first who understand the power of extending grace to others when they confess their own struggles.

Now, imagine the power of *that* kind of witness. Imagine the power of meekness in a world filled with pride, arrogance, strife, and power struggles. Imagine the power of a group of people who behave in such a countercultural way—who honor those who correct them, who understand the limits of their own knowledge, who are the first to confess their faults because they are safe in God's grace, who are eager to learn.

Imagine how such a people could heal a nation and draw others to their Jesus.

Application

Looking In

In order to become discerning people, we must learn to walk in meekness. This is especially difficult in a world that honors displays of power and sees humility as a liability. Because the temptation to trust in ourselves is ever present (and often rewarded!), we must become people sensitive to the Holy Spirit's conviction and correction.

1. In what specific areas do you find yourself tempted to trust your own strength, knowledge, commitment, or goodness? When are you most tempted to self-reliance?

2. How do you feel when someone offers you new information or corrects you? Why do you think you respond this way?

3. Which kinds of human leaders—a pastor or church leader, a politician, a spouse, a friend—do you find yourself trusting to fulfill the good things God has promised he will do for you? Who are you depending on in disproportionate ways?

4. Can you think of any characters in Scripture (or in your present life) who had to be corrected multiple times in their Christian journey? In what ways did their example and witness help you better understand the love of Christ, the power of the gospel, and the compassion of God?

5. Think of past times in your life when you assumed the posture of being "unchallengeable." How could you have handled the situation in better alignment with Jesus' countercultural call toward meekness?

Looking Up

It's hard to humble ourselves, but it's impossible without the hope of a loving, patient God who understands our weakness. In 1 Peter 5:5–6, Scripture promises that God resists the proud but gives grace the humble, and 1 John 1:9 tells us that those who confess their sins are safe with him. But more than this, Jesus himself endured suffering by trusting the Father: "When they hurled their insults at him, he did not retaliate; when he suffered, he made no threats. Instead, he entrusted himself to him who judges justly" (1 Pet. 2:23 NIV). Our ability to embrace meekness relies a great deal on whether we believe God is who he claims to be.

1. How easily and quickly can you confess your failures to God? How easily can you confess to others? In both cases, why do you think you can or cannot?

2. When you look at the example of how Jesus submitted himself to unjust suffering, does that encourage you or do you find it

uncomfortable? How is the idea of a meek Jesus at odds with your sense of who he is?

3. How does cultivating meekness support and prove our claims about the gospel? How does it reveal the character of God to a watching world?

4. Where do you specifically sense failure before God when it comes to his call to meek living? (For example, where have you been proud? Where have you cared more about winning than being godly?) How does Christ's work on the cross speak to that failure today?

5. Many times, we forget that the Lord is a safe and welcoming place to bring our weakness and failure. For the moments you feel the strong pull to retreat back into pride, what Bible verses can you keep nearby to aid you in remembering God's compassionate character and his desire to help you?

Looking Out

As you look at the world around you, the temptation to pride and self-reliance is everywhere. No person, family, ministry, political party, or group is immune from its corrupting influence, and in many ways, our culture even rewards it. But the risks of pride are incalculable, and ultimately it will destroy even the good things we hope to achieve.

1. Where have you seen pride at work in broader culture? How have you been taught to rely on yourself or human effort?

2. How have you seen pride sabotage relationships between people? How does self-reliance separate people and create division?

3. What would it take for our families, churches, and communities to become places where it is easy to confess our faults? What would we need to repent of for our communities to value meekness?

4. What people in your life might benefit if they saw you walk in this sort of correctable humility? How would your example of meekness challenge the typical expectations around being a "good Christian witness" and reveal the beauty of the gospel for what it offers?

5. If you lead other Christians in a group of some sort, would you say the group members understand Jesus as a meek person? Where do you see consistent expressions of pride in your group? What are some specific ways you can model meekness in your own leadership?

Looking Ahead

As followers of Jesus Christ, we have placed our hope for eternal salvation in Christ; this truth must inform our earthly hopes. Instead of striving in our own strength, we trust that God is at work fulfilling his promises to us. Instead of fighting for control of this earth, we pray "thy kingdom come" and trust him with the future. Because ultimately, we know that even if we never see the promises fulfilled in this life, it is not over. We believe that he will one day raise us to life again from the very earth that is our inheritance. His promise is sure and we hope in him.

1. Many people in the world around you do not have hope of life after death—they don't understand what it means to resurrect into eternity with God, and if they aren't in Christ, they will not inherit the earth. How might that affect the way they approach decisions in this earthly life? In what ways do you find yourself slipping into these same ways of thinking?

2. How should your hope of eternal life change how you navigate this life? In what specific ways does it set you apart from those who do not have this hope?

3. How does knowing that God will secure your future help you embrace meekness in the present?

4. Read 1 John 1:8–9. How does this passage both confront and comfort you in your pursuit of meekness?

5. Philippians 1:6 assures us that "he who started a good work in you will carry it on to completion until the day of Christ Jesus." How does knowing that God is at work in you, actively molding you to the image of Christ, encourage you as you pursue meekness?

Prayer of Confession and Commitment

Father, I confess that I put too much confidence in my own strength and intelligence. I know that I often depend on myself or other human beings instead of resting in your power. Teach me to humbly trust your care for me and let my actions and responses reflect Christ's own meekness and show forth the truth of the gospel. In Jesus' name, amen.

Chapter 5

HOLISTIC RIGHTEOUSNESS IN A WORLD THAT'S SELECTIVE

Jada Edwards

"Blessed are those who hunger and thirst for
righteousness, for they will be satisfied."
—Matthew 5:6 NASB

Have you felt desperate lately? Desperate for someone to understand you or your point of view? Desperate for civil agreement? Desperate for the church to be the guiding light it should be?

With so many "fires" being sparked and fueled on what seems like a daily basis, how can we not feel desperate? Desperate—hungry even—for a sign of hope. For things to change course and head toward some undefined (but deeply desired) better state.

I know, personally, there are realities that I truly wish were different. I wish the atmosphere around race relations wasn't so charged. I wish people who follow Christ were more consistent in character, grace, and truth. I wish that we could be civil enough to know how to disagree on politics and the challenges of a pandemic without losing friendships over our differences.

With all these desires and more, it would be fair to say I hunger for change. But I must be careful that as important as those things are, they are subject to both biblical truth and spiritual guidance. It's easy for our desires and desperations to dictate our ultimate appetite.

Wisdom Explained

We all have things we hunger for—things that we think will satisfy us. Many of those things are good, and there would be nothing wrong with us putting our effort toward them in order to see change. However, Matthew 5:6 teaches that when our deepest appetite is for the righteousness of God, only then are we satisfied. God's priorities and plans should always be our strongest pursuit. After all, this is the mark of a citizen of heaven, distinguishing us from citizens of the earth, according to Jesus. So . . . if this appetite offers evidence that we are truly in his kingdom—what in the world does it mean to hunger and thirst for righteousness?

Let's look at our verse. Two important ideas need to be noted here:

First, we are built to hunger and thirst. These are normal functions of the human body and of the human spirit. God not only expects that we hunger and thirst for something, he made us that way. Body and soul, Christian and non-Christian. Even most who've yet to find complete satisfaction in Jesus would still admit to being hungry and thirsty at a soul level. The desires in and of themselves aren't the issue. The point is that the God who loves you and created you knows exactly what will satisfy them.

Spiritually, these metaphors of being hungry and thirsty point to the "bread of life" (the name Jesus gives himself in John 6:35) and "living water" (a reference to the Holy Spirit in John 4:10 and John 7:38–39). Hunger and thirst both point to desperation. Here they're used metaphorically to illustrate that we should crave righteousness the same way we crave food and water as our most basic needs. When we choose Jesus as Lord, he satisfies our soul's craving and gives us eternal life (which only he can do) and in turn gives us a new appetite—*his* appetite—to be the driver of our everyday lives.

Second, righteousness should be what we hunger and thirst for. As Christians, this new appetite gives us a hunger different than that of the world. But what, exactly, is this new appetite? What is the new thing we now hunger for? "Righteousness."

What is righteousness? Well, that requires at least a two-part answer. First, *righteousness* is the condition of being acceptable to God as made possible by God. This is the *position* of righteousness God requires. To put it simply, God created us with a craving for him. We corrupted that craving with selfish appetites (Gen. 3) and passed on that corruption to every person at birth. With it came an eternal punishment, and the only answer was a perfect sacrificial substitute. Of course, we are far from perfection, so God provided a solution in Jesus Christ who makes us acceptable by paying for our sins and giving us his perfectly righteous record in exchange. When we exercise faith in Christ and his work on our behalf, we get to stand on that righteousness, which changes our *position* from deserving judgment to being *given* freedom and acceptance. Said another way, in Christ, we are finally and fully declared "righteous" in our position before God.

Second, once we are given this position by grace alone and through faith alone, we now have the capacity to *practice* righteousness. You could say it this way: because we *are* righteous before God because of Christ, and because we have been given a new appetite for righteousness, we now go out into the world and *do* righteous things. How? His power in us is what enables this capacity through the Holy Spirit. The righteousness of God is the standard of holiness to which God calls his people, which we see in his Word. We can also look to the life and character of Jesus Christ, for he is, according to John 1:14, "the Word [that] became flesh and dwelt among us." He came to rescue us and give us deep cravings for righteousness.

The Struggle

So why is all this talk about the position of righteousness and the practice of it so important? It's important because it's only *after* we have the position of righteousness—by faith in Christ—can we begin to crave the practice of righteousness in our lives.

If you have yet to completely surrender to Jesus Christ, you probably still have some cravings. But underneath those cravings, if you trace them down to the base level, you are likely struggling with something deep, something universal, something we all experience. You are craving the truest form of intimacy and connection. To be completely known and completely loved. Humanity had this for a minute in the garden of Eden before Adam and Eve sinned. This desire is normal and what most people spend their lives trying to realize.

I'm willing to bet you are looking to satisfy this desire in ways that haven't worked so far. Maybe you've done a lot of "good" things, or worked really hard, or tried to be available for people whenever you're needed. Maybe you've sought this intimacy in various kinds of relationships. You may not know it, but what you are really desiring is to know Jesus as Lord above all else. Why? Because he is the one who connects you to God so you can experience the intimacy that God originally intended to have with you. Our unrighteousness (sin) destroyed that intimacy in the beginning because God can't connect with sinful people. Jesus—the Divine Connector—is the only One who can restore what we destroyed. Because he is perfectly righteous, he's the only One who can give you the *position* of righteousness required to have relationship with God. There can be no life goal, no cultural cause, or altruistic ambition that should take priority over claiming positional righteousness through salvation. If you are in this undecided place, may I encourage you to save your energy in doing good things until you surrender to God?

And if you're a Christian and those you are influencing or praying for are unbelievers, please do them a favor and don't direct them to worthy causes without directing them to the cross. My heart breaks at the efforts of unbelievers, because while there may be some impact here on the earth, this is where it will end. Most importantly, my heart breaks because people who do noble and good things apart from submission to Christ will spend eternity separated from him, and there's no earthly pain that compares to that.

For those who are believers and followers of Christ, would you say the *practice* of righteousness is what you most crave? Jesus says it should be for all of us. Perhaps your answer is yes. So here's a follow-up question: What's the thing that came to your mind, the thing that proves you care about practicing righteousness in this world? If I had to guess, it's probably that one thing you really, deeply, and constantly care about—maybe something stemming from personal pain or experience. Is there an issue that you think if everyone "got it" all would be right—or at least much better—in the world? Whatever it is, it's probably not a wrong thing—in fact, it's likely a good thing. It probably reflects God's righteousness well in this world. But here's the struggle—it's also probably not the full picture of God's standard. See, Christ-followers are not exempt from illegitimately elevating *one* legitimately important issue and making it equivalent to *all* of God's righteousness. We can all struggle with the subtle danger of thinking *our* call to reflect God's righteousness is the *only* call there is—and we do this in different ways, depending on the circle we are in.

For example, some of us tend to make the ailments of humanity that speak deepest to our pains and passions unchallenged priorities, and in doing so, we neglect our holistic pursuit of righteousness. It could be advocacy for children—whether that's protection of the unborn or fighting for fairness in foster care and domestic violence or creating equal educational and economic opportunities. For others of us, especially with the increased exposure of long-standing tensions, we can be so vested in racial harmony that we isolate it as the *only* aspect of our spiritual appetites or the *only* way we fight for God's righteousness in the world. Still others of us swing the other way, only declaring God's righteousness and his great gospel in *word* and forgetting that God requires us to declare these things in *deed* as well (Matt. 5:16; 1 Thess. 2:8–12; James 1:22; 1 Pet. 2:12; 1 John 3:18; Rev. 19:8). Christians who struggle in this way spend time only talking of God's righteousness without living it out in our world, so that the world might see what it looks like. In other words, we can all fail to be holistic, making our issue *the only* issue, and in that failure lies the danger of self-righteousness. At this point you may be asking this question: Wait, aren't pursuits of unity, racial harmony, pervasive kindness, healing, forgiveness, justice, etc. all righteous things?

Yes. Those pursuits not only reflect the values and the character of Christ, they are reflections of God's righteousness demonstrated during the Old Testament as well. However, like I said before, a certain distortion can take over when we don't see each of those things as *aspects* of God's righteousness, or perhaps individual expressions of it, but instead view each of them as if it is the *absolute* standard or *full expression* of God's righteousness.

What Could It Look Like to Pursue a Full Picture of God's Righteousness?

Think about this conversation I had with a friend recently. To protect her privacy, let's call her Lena.

I noticed Lena's comment on the post of a mutual friend of ours (let's call her Crystal) and asked her about it. Crystal, a white woman, posted a request for people to pray for those in her family who were police officers since they risk their lives daily. At the time, a negative headline regarding an incident between police officers and a black man was the focus of all the news outlets. Lena, a black woman, was in a raw place of pain, passion, and frustration. Her comment on the post was harsh, to say the least. She basically questioned how any Christian could be thinking of police officers without also being burdened by what is happening to black men and women in America. That, of course, incited an extensive back-and-forth flurry of comments and debates. As with most commenters, some were well-meaning, seeking to understand, and many more were narrow-minded and downright hateful. This exchange was unhealthy, unloving, unnecessary (on that platform) and un-Jesus! I remember reading many of the comments, including Lena's, which was the fire-starter, wondering what good would come of this. I asked myself a series of questions: Is this helpful? Is this the right place? Is there a better option?

I decided to call Lena and share my struggle with her comment.

I have learned to focus my energy in relationships where I actually have influence, and not worry about changing people God hasn't given me influence with. And because I love my friend (and our mutual friend), we needed to have a conversation. Please note—a conversation was needed, not an additional comment to add fuel to the fire.

I called her to hear how she was doing. I wanted to understand her headspace before I offered any advice. (I recommend this order. Listen. Pray. Speak.) She shared the heaviness on her heart. We talked about the tension in being Christians and being black in America. There's so much pain that black people have experienced both collectively and personally. Sometimes it feels like a sharp cut, creating a fresh wound. But most often (for me anyway) it's like a chronic ache that you just get used to living with. Like most painful conditions, it feels good and therapeutic to connect with people who share your pain, and it is very easy to disconnect from those who don't.

Yet, as Christ-followers we have an identity that supersedes all others. We have a pursuit of righteousness that is all-encompassing and not isolated. Yes, justice is important to God (Amos 5:15, 24). Yes, reconciliation is at the heart of the gospel, so surely it's expected by those who claim to follow Jesus (2 Cor. 5:18). Specifically in America, Christians have much work to do when it comes to forgiveness, understanding, honesty, grace, and love between white people and people of color. No matter what ethnicity we are as believers, we have all chosen a path that directs us toward love even when we are in pain (John 15:13). A path that directs us to silence if we lack self-control (1 Cor. 9:27). When we hunger and thirst for righteousness, we hunger and thirst for ALL that Christ is, and we strive to obey the *whole* counsel of Scripture, not just the parts that support our side of things.

Lena and I wrapped up our conversation with the clear, although not easy, response to what had transpired. Lena needed to call Crystal and apologize—not for her feelings, pain, or passion. She needed to apologize for a response that was unloving and insensitive, not to mention public. She disregarded her friend's legitimate prayer need and elevated her own need to be heard and understood. In that moment,

Lena chose self-righteousness, born out of pain, over true righteousness. True righteousness demands that we demonstrate love and sympathy even when our own needs are unmet. As Christ-followers, we don't make ourselves the center of attention or demand that people serve our needs (Matt. 20:28), even if for noble and necessary reasons. Our hunger for God's righteousness checks our hearts when we are tempted to make our issue the only issue. And if we are unable to represent God well in the moment (Col. 4:6) we should remain silent. We bridle the tongue and pray (James 3:2). Practicing this kind of righteousness seems impossible, doesn't it? You're right. It is. Only Jesus Christ could do this! Surrendering to him as Lord means that practicing true righteousness *is* possible (Rom. 8:10; Gal. 2:20; Col. 1:27). Only people who have heaven's power can live in such heavenly wisdom when the hurts in our hearts are screaming to be heard.

After Lena and I talked and prayed and cried a little, she not only decided to apologize to Crystal but to have a transparent conversation with her about her pain as a black Christian woman in America. Before this conversation, Crystal had previously asked Lena how she was processing all the recent events and conversations around racial tension and Lena had dismissed her. Maybe she wasn't ready to talk about it or didn't have the energy to explain the well of her emotions and thoughts. But after posting that comment, Lena knew she needed to talk to her friend. She didn't want to miss any opportunities to point people to Jesus because of a comment made from a place of hurt.

Don't miss my point. Lena's pain is real and important; she should not deny it or water it down for someone else's comfort. She may even choose to join groups or church efforts to help foster godly conversations between believers who are hostile toward one another when it comes to race. But Lena knows as a Christ-follower, even her deepest pain takes second place to the relentless pursuit of true and holistic righteousness.

Sometimes our pain isn't what gets in the way, it's our fear. Or even our pride.

Now let me introduce you to another friend of mine. She's a leader in the local church and has a long-standing itinerant ministry (teaching all over the world). Let's call her Natalie. She loves God's Word, she is obeying his call to fight poverty in our world, and she also happens to be white. Remember she's a friend, so her understanding of what is happening in our culture should be more than distantly investigative. She's known me for many years, but recently when tensions began to rise between black and white Christian leaders, bringing new exposure to racial divisions, she stayed silent. I don't mean she didn't volunteer to use her platform to speak biblical, albeit controversial truth, into these spaces. (After all, to not post on social media or speak on a platform about racial matters on a daily basis does not mean a person isn't working toward Christian unity in their daily life.) I mean when Natalie was *asked* to be a part of a discussion among church leaders—when God *teed her up*—to share personal perspectives and think through how to make progress toward biblical unity, she declined.

Now, before you think I'm being unreasonable, I have pretty realistic expectations about what people will choose to take on as a cause. We are ALL self-centered and self-serving by nature. On top of that, we all have different callings, and none of us can speak to every single issue in every single moment (nor should we try). So, I don't have any demands as to how other people respond to the issues in our world. But when Natalie said *why* she declined the opportunity (remember—I wanted to listen first), she told me she didn't want to get in the "messiness" of things. When I asked her why she didn't have a problem getting in the messiness of the poverty in politically charged countries, she didn't have an answer. Trust me, this was not an antagonistic conversation. It was an authentic one between friends. I would expect her to challenge me in the same way.

I struggled with Natalie's dismissal of the opportunity. If she declined because she believed there were people who are better qualified or have more authority on this issue, that would have been a different motive altogether. I struggled instead because not only did I sense that her decision was based in fear, I also thought she was elevating her individual call to righteousness over God's fuller picture of righteousness—especially when he seemed to be *asking* her to do the latter. Righteousness is not only fighting systemic poverty; it is speaking and embodying biblical truth whenever we have the opportunity to do it—especially if God is the One who creates the opportunity. I didn't want Natalie to abandon her God-given mission in favor of something I cared about—we need her work in the world!—but I did think this could be a wonderful chance for her to point to a fuller picture of God's righteousness since the opportunity sought her out. We talked a while and she never changed her answer about that opportunity. I was disappointed, but I didn't choose to dissolve our friendship. We're friends, not twins! I didn't doubt her love for God; we just didn't agree on this.

A few weeks passed and another similar opportunity was presented to her by a different group. This time she accepted. Natalie called to tell me she had said "yes," and admitted she was a little scared to say the wrong thing. She felt insecure and unsure of her qualifications. So I did my best to encourage her and remind her that a love for God and compassionate boldness for his truth wouldn't fail her. I was thankful for my friend's courage and knew God would cover her.

Lena and Natalie represent just a couple of countless moments that we must choose God's values over our own validation. There is a time and place to express our passions, advocate for good causes, and even debate their biblical *rightness*. But biblical rightness does not mean that our issues become the epitome of God's *righteousness*.

Lena and Natalie had many cravings—valid ones. But their actions proved that deeper than those personal cravings, they ultimately craved a full picture of God's righteousness. And what did that lead to? Blessing. Lena and her friend built a new bridge between the two of them. Natalie now has a clear conscience, even if her confidence is shaky as she seeks to more fairly and fully represent God's truth in her ministry. Though it does not mean things aren't hard or uncomfortable, both women are flourishing more now than they were before because they chose to live into the picture of what God's kingdom truly looks like, giving the world a preview of that future day when God's people will be satisfied by the total state of righteousness in the world. It shouldn't surprise us that Jesus was right all along: *Blessed* are those who hunger and thirst for righteousness, for they will be satisfied.

By the power of God in us, let's increase our appetites for—and then let's practice—*all* that God says is righteous. For when we do, we show the citizens of earth—those who only know either self-righteousness or partial righteousness—what a true and full picture of *God's* righteousness looks like.

Application

Looking In

Stirring up our hunger for righteousness is no easy feat. Trying to *act* differently is one thing, stirring up new *appetites* is entirely something different. In a culture that is constantly suggesting what we should desire, pursuing what pleases God will definitely be unpopular at times.

1. What beliefs or behaviors stir up the deepest passion in you? What breaks your heart? Do you think this issue(s) is so close to your heart that it may have become your measurement for righteousness?

2. How do you feel and/or respond when someone doesn't understand your hurt or see the world through your eyes?

3. Do you have genuine friends that think differently from you? Are you regularly around people who are passionate about issues different from yours?

4. How often are you deeply affected by the evils of this world that have no personal or direct impact on you? How do you respond when you encounter these issues? (Prayer? Action?)

Looking Up

A steady diet for Scripture and prayer will no doubt stir up our appetite for God's righteousness. Sometimes we can get stuck in familiar passages, our "go-to" verses and we find our prayer life stagnant. Without constant communication with God, we will fall into a narrow-minded perspective.

1. How often do you study/meditate on Scripture? Not simply reading Scripture, but delighting in it like Psalm 1:2 tells us to?

2. How often do you study/meditate on unfamiliar passages of Scripture? Do you skip over what seems uninteresting, irrelevant, or hard to understand?

3. Are you prayerful before responding to people or replying/commenting on something? (Colossians 4:6 says we need to be Spirit-led for each moment.) Why or why not?

4. How often do you pray for God to show you how he sees the world, people, and the brokenness around us? How often do you confess when you've held a personal position as the ultimate position?

Looking Out

Ultimately this new hunger and new thirst should change the way we love people. We shouldn't see people as projects that need work but as carriers of different passions and appetites. We should connect with others on a human level and love them on a spiritual level—even if they don't reciprocate that love. God created us for relationship, so we must work to love others well even when it's uncomfortable.

1. Are you able to view people that do things you "would never do" with compassion? Why or why not?

2. We all are all sinners, but our upbringing, passions, and resources can greatly impact how we *express* those sins. How have you seen this to be true in your own life and the lives of those around you?

3. Do you initiate conversations to gain understanding on how others think? Do you offer your perspectives in a way that doesn't belittle others (even subtly)?

4. Are you able to redirect unhealthy conversations toward something that honors God even when beliefs differ? If you're the reason a conversation takes a turn toward unhealthy or hurtful, are you able to apologize or initiate reconciliation?

5. If you lead other Christians in some sort of group, consider your participants. Where do you see selective righteousness at play? How might you move toward holistic righteousness as a group?

Looking Ahead

Not only did God create us for relationship, he commissions us as believers (assigns us) to use relationships as a vehicle for gospel conversations. We should be slow to judge character and quick to pray for Christ to transform hearts. Our greatest goal can't be limited to the resolution of a few issues—our greatest goal must be the constant presentation of the gospel.

1. Do you ask God for gospel opportunities as you engage with people—whether they are friends or strangers? (Sometimes these

opportunities are a full-on presentation of the gospel, but most often they are best met with a thought-provoking question or well-placed nugget of truth. Jesus did this masterfully in conversation with the Samaritan woman in John 4.)

2. Do you find your heart yearning more to grow the army of believers or to grow an audience for a particular issue?

3. For a moment, picture Jesus' kingdom that will come in full one day, in the new heavens and new earth. What is the first thing you think of, or what excites you most? Is it the fact that all the people there will be perfectly loving and living out God's righteousness, every moment of every day? If that wasn't the first thing that excited you about God's coming kingdom, why do you think that's the case? What does this exercise tell you about what your heart craves most?

Prayer of Confession and Commitment

God, thank you for the gift of righteousness available by believing in the work and life of Jesus Christ and surrendering to him as Lord. Please stir up an appetite in me consistent with that gift. Help me to pursue the whole counsel of your truth and give me a hunger for holiness and right living in every area of my life. Help me to see where my self-righteousness or selective righteousness has crept in, and realign me. Give me a heart for people that is greater than my perspective. Give me courage and compassion to engage in gospel conversations. Amen.

Chapter 6

MERCY IN A WORLD OF SCROOGES

Ashley Marivittori Gorman

"Blessed are the merciful,
for they will be shown mercy."
—Matthew 5:7

After twenty-six hours of labor, Cole (my husband) and I were thrilled when our daughter, Charlie, was finally in our arms. She was beautiful. Precious. Ours. I was full of excitement as I anticipated the months ahead. Long, lazy days together with my baby. Snuggling in her rocking chair. Cooing and laughing and enjoying the bright rays of summer together.

But the summer never got bright. At least not for me. As the days passed, my bright and shiny normal got grayer and foggier. Charlie wouldn't stop crying. And eventually, the same was true for me. The tears streaming down my face at all hours of the day were new to me. So was the aimlessness I felt when I'd walk around the neighborhood pushing the stroller, the cries radiating from it around my ears, ringing out like they had for weeks.

See, I'm a "power through" person. No matter how hard life is, my way of approaching things has always been to get your game face on, put your head down, and get through it. But the months following Charlie's birth—well, I couldn't power through them. The only thing I felt was fear—deep, consuming, white-hot fear that I couldn't explain or see out of—mixed with a fog that wouldn't lift. I was terrified all the time, on the verge of screaming but without the energy to open my mouth. *Something is wrong with her,* I would think. *Something's wrong . . . something's wrong.* The chorus would repeat over and over.

After weeks of this, Cole found me hidden away, crying in our closet with the lights off. Strong, spirited, and thick-skinned just months before, I was now a weakling, a puddle of tears. I had tried to keep it all from him—I so badly wanted to be a good, put-together mom and wife. I wanted that sweet, vibrant, fun story so many other moms had with their newborns. But Cole found me right smack-dab in that story's evil twin—unraveled and desperate in the dark.

He turned the light on. I expected a look of disappointment or perhaps a five-point plan on how to get my personality back again. I tried to piece together some sort of explanation—"I'm sorry, *I'm so sorry* . . . I don't know what's wrong with . . ." Mid-sentence, eyes lowered in shame and terror, I felt a tender hand beneath my chin, lifting it up. My eyes looked up fearfully through the tears to meet his, which instead of disappointment, held more tears than mine did. "Honey, goodness, I should have realized how hard this has been for you—why have you been bearing this all alone? Come here." Compassion and concern flickered in his eyes as his arms scooped me up.

I didn't know what to say in that moment. I was bewildered by this man who lifted my head in the darkness, cried along with me, and held me close. I had never experienced his tenderness to this level before, and not because he wasn't a tender person up till then, but because I never really needed a reason to take him up on it. I sat there and leaned into him for a while, sobbing.

It wasn't long before I was bewildered again—this time, by my sister-in-law, Alyssa, who showed up on our doorstep to help us. And by "showed up" I mean *moved in*. She could have stopped by sporadically while keeping a safe distance from the crazy, but she didn't. She chose to come near, to dwell with us right in the middle of the fear and fog.

Wisdom Explained

After directing his listeners to crave righteousness in his famous sermon, Jesus calls them—and us—to cultivate mercy: "Blessed are the merciful, for they will be shown mercy."

Jesus points out that the kind of person who flourishes[1] in this life—and the kind of person who is genuinely a citizen of his kingdom and will one day inherit it in full—is one who is reflexively compassionate, tender, and kind toward others in their misery or affliction. When we look at the places where mercy and compassion are mentioned in Scripture, the original language reveals to us that these are not merely emotions that can stay stuffed inside, but stir so deeply on the gut-level that they compel a response on the action level. In other words, mercy can't stay put. It moves. This means a faithful Christian should have such a constant, visceral compassion toward others that she is ready to help at any moment, springing toward anyone—friend or foe—caught in pain, harm, struggle, or sin.[2] As Sinclair Ferguson would say, "Mercy is getting down on your hands and knees and doing what you can to restore dignity to someone whose life has been broken by sin."[3]

That all sounds well and good on a coffee mug, but when we sit back and observe the knee-jerk reactions of most people in our world (especially when conversing about a controversial topic or the news of someone's recent failure), mercy is nowhere to be found. The prevailing

---

[1] I am indebted to Jonathan Pennington's book *The Sermon on the Mount and Human Flourishing* for framing the Beatitudes in terms of flourishing as opposed to modern-day notions of blessing.

[2] Here, I used various lexicons (Brown-Driver-Briggs, Strong's, Thayer's, etc.) along with a Hebrew-Greek Study Bible which all offer helpful insight into Strong's NT entries 1656: ἔλεος, 1655: ἐλεήμων, 4697: σπλαγχνίζομαι, 4698: σπλάγχνα, and 7349: מוּתְר. Also used: *The Greek New Testament, Fifth Revised Edition with Dictionary*, 2016.

[3] Sinclair Ferguson, *The Sermon on the Mount: Kingdom Life in a Fallen World* (Edinburgh: Banner of Truth, 1988), 31.

wisdom of our fallen world isn't tenderness; it's harshness. It says that the way to get ahead in life is to pull it together, toughen up, and get over it already. That people don't need a handout or a good cry; they need a swift kick in the rear. That the way to respond to that mommy war on social media is in all caps, guns blazing, because kindness is for the birds—or people who have no convictions. That nice guys finish last, and that the best way to handle the betrayals or failures of others is to get even. That as sad as the Tiny Tims of the world are, the cold hard truth is that they'll get weeded out eventually—that only the Scrooges survive.

Who Are You Calling a Scrooge?

Perhaps at this point you're thinking, *Yeah, the Scrooges out there are the worst. But I'm a pretty decent person in the mercy category. I get teary-eyed at those commercials about the less fortunate. And you should see me around the holidays—I lose it in every single Hallmark movie!*

Fair enough. Those commercials get me too. But I'm not talking about those fleeting moments. I'm talking about those daily, relentless, you've-got-to-be-kidding-me kind of interactions with these sorts of people:

- The classroom parent who *always* forgets when it's their turn to bring snacks, forcing us to cover *again*.
- The family member who finds a way to insult us through a compliment.
- The boss who needs us to take on more, even though she hasn't given us a pat on the back in *years*.
- The gal at the gym who takes too long to use the equipment.
- Those neighbors who make us want to sprint inside and shut the blinds when we see them

coming to shake their finger at us for who-knows-what this time.

- The toddler who screams "Mom" for the twenty-seventh time in the last three minutes.
- The gal in our small group who clearly can't get the memo that she has to *actually show up*.
- The friend who asks our advice for the same old issue and never takes it.
- The husband who forgot to pick up his socks or was late to pick up the kids. *Again.*
- The friend who is blind to the fact that at least she has a husband to begin with while the rest of us deal with the insanity of dating apps.
- Those moms in the online forums—you know, the ones who are straight-up fools for their stance on cloth diapers vs. disposable ones. Or Young Living essential oils vs. doTerra. Or public school vs. homeschooling. Or full-time work vs. staying at home. Or, heaven help us, *vaccines*.

See, I'm not talking about empathy for Hallmark characters. I'm talking about real life. I'm talking about the expectations we hold over our marriages, friendships, or ministry participants, keeping score of every failure or infraction just in case we need it for ammo later. Or the screen shots we send our favorite snarky text thread when a common enemy fails or makes a fool of themselves, and we enjoy laughing at them. Or the way we scroll past the consistent cry for help we've been noticing in that one girl's feed over the past couple months because *oh, cute, look at those shoes on my favorite influencer in the next post*. Or the memes we share that belittle some other tribe we don't like. Or the way we interrupt and overpower our spouse in a group conversation when he's getting the story wrong and we could probably tell it better. Or the way we mentally ruminate on an argument that's long gone now, imagining the killer comeback we should have said to really stick it to them.

I could go on, but I have a feeling you get the picture. If someone observed you in every single one of those scenarios, would they report that your consistent response—in both heart and deed—was *mercy*? Tenderness? An unstoppable readiness to offer compassion toward the other party?

Right. Me neither.

Getting Desperate

Three months after Charlie's birth, the dark fog and the fear lifted, little by little. Until one night I realized Charlie had a fever. Within just a few minutes, it went from low-grade to surging. She started to make strange grunting sounds. Her arms extended outward like a scarecrow, moving up and down in a jerky, odd way, and her sweet blue eyes looked past me, staring off into nowhere.

The dormant chorus erupted with a vengeance: *Something's wrong. Something's wrong. Something's wrong.* In one of those primal-mama-bear moments, I picked Charlie up, flew downstairs, and tore out the front door and into the car.

We made it to the hospital. I broke through the doors, screaming. All over again, I was a woman unraveling at the seams. My child was seizing in my arms, and I had no resources to bring her to the other side of this safely. She was sick. I was helpless. Bleary-eyed. Shaking. Desperate. Through the tears, I could make out, ever so slightly, a man across the lobby clothed in white, looking through some papers in his hands.

I ran as fast as my feet could carry me without dropping Charlie. I pushed his papers down, pulled at his sleeve, and locked eyes with him. The tears ran down, red hot, and my voice cracked. "Help us! Help her." He looked down to see Charlie. I kept on. "She's . . . she's seizing. I don't know how . . . I can't . . . *Please. Please help us.*"

Long story short, after a weeklong stay in the hospital, we discovered that I was right all along—something *was* wrong. In very simply terms, Charlie had been in septic shock due to a kidney condition we had no prior knowledge of. And praise be to God, she made it through and is doing just fine now.

There's a reason I went to a hospital instead of a bank or a post office on that fitful night. I didn't need a banker or a postal worker. I needed someone who could *heal*.

As I read the Bible, I find I'm not alone. We find similar people in the Gospels—desperate types who follow Jesus around like the blind, the Gentile, the ill, the demon-oppressed, and the leper (Matt. 9:27; 15:22; 20:30–31; Luke 17:11–13). They make similar statements to the one I made to that doctor, wailing in their need: "Have mercy on us, Son of David!" Jesus has a term for them: sick. Listen to his words: "Healthy people don't need a doctor—sick people do. I have come to call not those who think they are righteous, but those who know they are sinners" (Mark 2:17 NLT). To better understand his point, let's consider a story he tells:

> [Jesus] also told this parable to some who trusted in themselves that they were righteous and looked down on everyone else: "Two men went up to the temple to pray, one a Pharisee and the other a tax collector. The Pharisee was standing and praying like this about himself: 'God, I thank you that I'm not like other people—greedy, unrighteous, adulterers, or even like this tax collector. I fast twice a week; I give a tenth of everything I get.' But the tax collector, standing far off, would not even raise his eyes to heaven but kept striking his chest and saying, 'God, have *mercy* on me, a sinner!'
>
> "I tell you, this one went down to his house justified rather than the other, because everyone who exalts himself will be humbled, but the one who

humbles himself will be exalted." (Luke 18:9–14, emphasis added)

Do you hear the defense the Pharisee builds for himself in the presence of God? That's what we do sometimes, don't we? *Oh Lord, thank you I'm not like those people! Thank you for making me so decent—I go to church, I cry during Hallmark movies, I even give to random charities on Facebook.*

Who are "those people" for you? If you could fill in the blank, who would you say is ruining our country, or threatening the health of the church? If you could point to people who are the real problem these days, who would be on the other side of your finger?

If the primary face coming to mind right now isn't your own, Jesus says you're the Pharisee—the one who can't receive mercy because he defends himself against it. Do you see how he rolls out a laundry list of ways he's been a decent chap, proving he doesn't need mercy because he's doing just fine on his own? He knows that sinners exist out there, but he won't admit he's one of them. He's smug. Standing next to the tax collector, he's Scrooge. He can't extend mercy to the guy praying next to him because he won't experience it for himself.

On the other hand, the tax collector (hated by the Jews for being not only greedy, but betrayers) doesn't compare himself to anyone. He simply admits what's going on in his own heart before the Lord, and calls out for healing and help. Arms beating his own chest instead of crossed in defense, all the man did was throw himself on the mercy of God—no rationalizing, no turned-up nose, no assuming he was better than the other guy who was praying. And that mercy he called for, it found him, and lifted his chin. Walking in, he's a lowly sinner. Walking out, he's justified before God and exalted in the sight of heaven. All because he was willing to admit the truth that he wasn't decent, he was sick.

Here's Jesus' point: the riches of God's mercy can only be poured out on those who uncross their arms, unroll their eyes, and simply tell the truth that something's wrong inside—that the problem with the world isn't "them," it's *me*. Put another way, the only people who don't get to experience the lavish tenderness and mercy of God are those who defend themselves against it. And in doing so, because they haven't experienced the warmth of his mercy for themselves, they stay cold-hearted toward others.

In a world that is trained to cross its arms and justify itself, Jesus' other-worldly wisdom is genius: Want to be merciful? Admit you're a Scrooge. And then throw yourself on the mercy of God. Break in the doors, unhinged and desperate. Lock eyes with the Healer clothed in white. Run to the One who has the power to turn a stone heart to flesh, a cold heart warm, a hard heart soft. Don't craft some explanation. Don't list off all the reasons you're better than the next guy. Just tell him you're sick. *He'll make you new.*

But What about Judgment and Justice?

Common questions arise when we talk about God's mercy in these ways. What about justice? Doesn't the Bible also speak of God's judgment and wrath for sin? It certainly does. And the beauty of Christianity is that it allows room for both mercy and justice to coincide, no place more than the cross of Christ.

Justice requires scores to be settled. Sins have to be handled. To leave them swept under the rug, with no accountability, is wrong. And so God rightly demands atonement. The justice of the cross is that all your sin really does get paid for in the end, fair and square. Accountability is achieved. But the mercy of the cross is that it doesn't get paid for by *you*. God's compassion was so great that when he saw your sin—even when you were too blind to see it yourself—he redirected all the wrath it deserved toward himself. Even while you were his enemy, God reflexively sprinted ahead of you to take your place in the person of Christ. Why? Because he'd rather cover all your sins with his own blood than watch you suffer. That's the gospel: your sins are fully atoned for (justice), but not by you (mercy). The cross of

Christ—there's no greater display of justice served and mercy poured out at the exact same time.

How We Change

If you and I are anything like the disciples, we forget just how compassionate God is. We may have run to him for mercy in our conversion, but we forget to run to him for mercy every single day after that. So how do we remember? How do we receive mercy daily, so that we can extend mercy to everyone around us—even "those people" who drive us crazy? How do we stay soft when the current of our culture tells us to be hard?

First, we *behold*. Scripture reveals that not only does everyone have some sort of god they worship, but everyone *becomes* like the god they fix their gaze on (Pss. 115:4–8; 135:15–18; 2 Cor. 3:18). So, if we want to become more like the God of Mercy, we must behold him in all his splendor throughout the Bible. When we do, we realize that, start to finish, he is marked by mercy. From his graciousness in creating a world for us to enjoy, to his immediate response to his fallen children in the garden, to his plans for blessing the whole world through his chosen people, to his incessant pursuit of his wayward people through the prophets, to becoming human so that he could reach toward us in compassion with his own bare hands—hands that would stretch out across a cross to pay for all our waywardness once and for all—to the invitation to live once again in a world finally set right, the God of the Bible is inconceivably kind. The Bible presents God as One who sees exactly who you are, right in the middle of your sin, rebellion, blindness, and fist raised against him, and comes running toward you anyway. Like Alyssa, instead of staying away from the crazy, he moves in with it. Like Cole, he sees you in the darkness, and can't bear to leave you alone there. And so he comes close to you in the person of Jesus, the Light of the World. "Because of our God's merciful compassion," Zechariah says, he chose to "shine on those who live in darkness" (Luke 1:78–79a). The God of the Bible is the only god in all of religious history who doesn't make us work our way up to him, but comes down, finds us in our darkest place, turns the lights on, and scoops us up. It is no wonder why many scholars consider God's mercy his most fundamental attribute.[4]

Next, we *experience*. It's one thing to read about the God of Mercy in the Bible. It's another thing to take him up on it in real time. That's what faith is—taking God up on what he says about himself. That's what the tax collector did. And his example for us is not just something we should experience in conversion, but every day after that. Consider Hebrews 4. It teaches that those of us in Christ can approach God's throne in boldness. Wonderful. So, now that we're finally there, unafraid and bold before God's throne because of Christ who made a way for us to approach it, what exactly are we supposed to . . . *do* there? "Therefore, let us approach the throne of grace with boldness, *so that we may receive mercy* and find grace to help us in time of need" (Heb. 4:16, emphasis added). Do you see it? One act of mercy on the cross made way for you to enjoy a million more moments of mercy. You need somewhere to throw all the worry, frustration, anger, bitterness, pain, and even joy that come with everyday life—that's what God's throne is for. *Giving you a soft place to land with all that stuff is why he brought you to himself in the first place.* You don't have to power through on your own. Your God is not annoyed that you're back yet again with new needs. His mercy can't run out of steam, and he *longs* to extend it to you (Lam. 3:22–23; Isa. 30:18 NASB). Take God up on that. Let him lift your head.[5]

If we hit a season where we're especially quick to snap at others, harsh in spirit toward those we don't agree with, or naturally defensive, we must consider this an indicator that either we haven't beheld

---

[4] Here, I am thinking of folks like Craig Blomberg in his commentary on Matthew (*The New American Commentary: An Exegetical and Theological Exposition of Holy Scripture, NIV Text*), Dane Ortlund in his book *Gentle and Lowly*, and various early church fathers.

[5] For more on this, see Dane Orlund's *Gently and Lowly*, chapter 3. Actually, just read the whole book.

the God of Mercy in the Scriptures, or we haven't taken him up on that mercy in a long time. If that's true for you, take heart. The solution for harshness is not to beat yourself up or even try harder—it's to run to the throne. It's to enjoy fresh mercy, over and over and over. Friend, don't defend against the mercy that could change you all the way through. *Throw yourself on it.* Often. And over time, you'll find you're thawing out, you're warming up, you're more tender in spirit, you're willing to draw near to the people you once hated. Instead of sick in heart toward others, you're getting healthier and healthier. This is what God's mercy does. It heals us back into the image of what humans were always supposed to be.

Mercy for Brothers and Betrayers Alike

Over time, Christians growing in mercy will become less and less offendable. But that does not mean that a Christian never deals with the sins committed against them. Should a brother or sister sin against us in a way that cuts deep or continues to linger in our mind and heart, we're told to first examine ourselves to see what *we're* contributing to the problem and then seek out the other party directly so that we might point out the offense on their end, hopefully correcting the problem (Matt. 7:3–5; 18:15).

Yet even this process of correction is soaked in mercy, as Galatians 6:1–2 teaches us. "If someone is overtaken in any wrongdoing, you who are spiritual, restore such a person with a gentle spirit, watching out for yourselves so that you also won't be tempted. Carry one another's burdens, so fulfill the law of Christ." Here we see that mercy does not mean avoiding corrective conversations; it means we correct in ways that are diametrically opposed to the way the world does. When we encounter a brother or sister caught in idiocy, folly, or even betrayal toward us, we do not bare our teeth and lash out, cancel them, or relish their failure. Instead, we correct them gently, through tears instead of anger, because you know what? We've been there before and we could easily be there again.

The way a Christian responds to a sinner—brother and betrayer alike—is to get on our hands and knees beside them as they break under the weight of sin, trying to help raise it off of them, so that they can lift their head enough to look around and see the horrors of what they've been doing. And even when they vex us in the process, even when they sin against us, we beg God that the wrath for those sins would not fall on their head, but the head of the Savior, whose blood stands ready to protect them from harm, as it did us. We remain "kind to one another, tenderhearted, forgiving one another, just as God in Christ forgave you" (Eph. 4:32 ESV). After all, we were met with his unfathomable mercy at our worst. How could we then turn around and be cruel to our neighbor at theirs? Or put in Jesus' logic, how could we be forgiven a mountain of debt only to then hold our neighbor hostage for a buck fifty (Matt. 18:21–35)? Ultimately, even when our neighbor genuinely wounds us, we do not return evil for evil because we know the truth: our enemies, oppressors, and betrayers cannot see what they are doing in their foolishness, and retaliation has no power to open the eyes of the blind or change the heart of a foe (Rom. 12:17–21).

Meet Me at the Charcoal Fire

If you're looking for a biblical example of this, consider Peter who infamously denied his Lord three times in a row. The gospel of John tells us exactly where this happened. Around a "charcoal fire" (John 18:18) in a courtyard outside of the high priest's house, where Jesus was being questioned and beaten (Luke 22:54–65). What's worse is that in the moment of Peter's denial—as Jesus braves interrogation, beatings, and mockery just inside the high priest's house—Jesus turns his gaze from his oppressors and locks eyes with Peter across the courtyard (Luke 22:61). He *watches* Peter betray him. Can you imagine? We all have past places of failure. Peter's was this charcoal fire. And when he realized what he'd done in this place, the shame was too much to bear. He ran away from the fire and wept bitterly (Luke 22:62).

A charcoal fire only shows up twice in the gospel of John. We just encountered the first instance—the place of Peter's threefold betrayal. And where do we find the other? In the scene of Peter's threefold restoration. After his crucifixion and resurrection, the risen Christ appears to his disciples who are fishing. He beckons them to the shoreline. "When they got out on land, they saw a charcoal fire there, with fish lying on it, and bread. . . . 'Come and have breakfast,' Jesus told them" (John 21:9, 12). The last time Peter met Jesus' gaze over a charcoal fire was the moment of his betrayal. And now the risen Savior invites him back to that place of failure, this time locking eyes with him over breakfast and brotherhood and laughter. That's mercy. Immediately after eating around that fire, Jesus speaks directly with Peter, telling him to feed his sheep (Jn. 21:15-17).

In essence, Jesus' point is this: *as I just fed you in the place of your failure, so you must feed others. My sheep will need you to guide them through their woes and lapses and hardheartedness, their charcoal fires, so when you come across their needs or wrongheadedness, show them the mercy I just showed you. When they stray and betray, point them to the cross and bring them breakfast.*

Do you see? Jesus took Peter's place of failure, betrayal, and bitter weeping, and turned it into a place of abundance from which he could minister to others. From here on, the charcoal fire would not represent the dark days in Peter's mind. It would represent the place where mercy poured out. In the very place Peter starved Jesus of the dignity and honor he deserved, Jesus handed those things back to him. This is what returning good for evil looks like, and it is impossible without the example, power, and spirit of Christ.

In the end, we see that a swift kick in the rear is not what turned Peter the Great Betrayer into Peter the Great Apostle. Mercy did. If you are wondering how in the world to handle a betrayal or an enemy, look to Christ and remember that mercy isn't weaker than judgment, it's actually stronger. It bewilders the enemy, stopping them in their tracks and lowering their guard, so that their heart might be exposed to the transformative power of the gospel. Justice and judgment are indeed necessary. But where judgment can settle a score, only mercy can change a person from the inside out. Justice rights the wrong done, but mercy rights the wrongdoer. And so if you're trying to win over an enemy (and let's say this enemy truly *is* in the wrong), remember the way God won you over. It was his kindness that led you to repentance (Rom. 2:4). Choosing to extend mercy to an enemy who genuinely needs to repent is not backing away from the fight or going soft; it's picking up the only weapon powerful enough to pierce the heart.

As it turns out, Jesus shows us time and time again the best way to fight fire isn't with fire, but with warmth. May we run toward that warmth daily at his throne, bask in it till the point of overflow, and then pour it out on others, friend and foe alike. May we walk into his throne room a Scrooge, and walk out like our Savior.

> But love your enemies, and do good, and lend, expect-
> ing nothing in return, and your reward will be great,
> and you will be sons of the Most High, for he is kind
> to the ungrateful and the evil. Be merciful, even as your
> Father is merciful. (Luke 6:35–36)

Application

Looking In

1. Think back to a time when you encountered mercy in a way you didn't expect. How did you respond?

2. In what ways do you defend yourself against the mercy of God sometimes? Why do you think you do this?

3. Do you reflexively draw near to sinners and sufferers? Why or why not? What person or types of people do you find yourself consistently recoiling from?

4. What situations or relationships tend to tempt you toward a response of snarkiness or harshness? Where do you typically return evil for evil, falling back into the worldly wisdom of retaliation? What does this response reveal about your view of God?

Looking Up

1. According to this chapter's exploration of Hebrews 4, what is waiting for you when you approach God's throne? How does that change your view of the Christian life?

2. Explain how God's justice and mercy are displayed simultaneously on the cross.

3. In what ways have you viewed God as a Scrooge? Why do you think you've done this? How does the Bible speak to this view?

4. What is your charcoal fire—your place of greatest failure? Have you ever let God meet you in that place with mercy?

Looking Out

1. Where do you see a lack of mercy in our culture? Be specific.

2. In which relationships within your family are you unwilling to show mercy? Within your neighborhood? Within your church? Your child's school? Online? How might you take a step toward showing mercy to those people this week?

3. Consider the ways others have failed you in this season—identify their charcoal fires. Instead of ignoring the failure or seething over it, how might you meet them in that place of failure and return good for evil?

4. If you lead a group of Christians, would you say the posture of your group as a whole is a merciful one? Consider your own leadership—in what ways could you be a better model of mercy to those in your group? How might you equip members to grow in this area? (Idea: Read the Old Testament story of Jonah together as a group, and consider why, at the end of the story, Jonah spurns the mercy God wants to extend to his enemies [Jonah 4:1–4]. Wrestle through the implications of the story together).

Looking Ahead

1. What does living mercifully show unbelievers about the kingdom of God?

2. Do you ever think being tender and kind is too mushy? How does that square with the culture of the new heavens and earth? In what ways is God preparing you for that future reality?

Prayer of Confession and Commitment

God, I confess I've been following earthly patterns of harshness and retaliation. I have grown cold in heart, and I can see the ways it is affecting my posture toward others. I have forgotten just how compassionate you are! I confess that instead of taking you up on the mercy you want to lavish on me, I've defended myself against it. I run into your throne room right now and ask you for fresh compassion, help, and strength. Help me to keep running to you with my needs, sins, and worries, and in doing so, change me into a person who is reflexively tender toward both sinners and saints. Amen. 🔥

Chapter 7

A SINGULAR FOCUS IN AN UNFOCUSED WORLD

Jasmine Holmes

"Blessed are the pure in heart,
for they will see God."
—Matthew 5:8

I can't play a lick of chess.

And it's not for lack of trying. I remember sitting in an older relative's home in front of the board, fingers itching to understand the game, trying to listen patiently as a wizened distant cousin expounded upon the complex network of rules. I nodded, picking up each piece . . . and proceeded to play a game of checkers.

My own chess illiteracy notwithstanding, when Netflix released *The Queen's Gambit*—a period drama about a fictional chess genius— I was hooked by her endless strategizing. The idea that this woman could think two, three, ten moves into the future astounded me and renewed my inner eight-year-old's hankering to understand the complexity of one of the oldest pastimes.

Beth thought of *everything*.

Lo and behold, after several hours of binging Beth Harmon's every move . . . I still can't play a lick of chess.

But the lure of a game of strategy still calls to me. And luckily (or, unluckily, as I'm soon to argue), we don't need to understand the complexities of a chess game to get that master strategist feeling—all we need to do is log onto the internet.

The Sway of the Media

The rooks and pawns, kings and queens of my ideal chess game have been replaced with lots of things these days, but what strikes me most is the way they've been replaced with the swirl of likes, shares, saves, and retweets of social media. Myriad chess strategy handbooks can be replaced with a precursory understanding of how to have an argument on the internet. We can stalk our feeds like a chess master watches the board, planning our next move before our opponent has even taken his hand off of the rook—or, in this case, the mouse.

You've likely already seen many examples of this in previous chapters of this book, and that makes sense, because the way most people engage with each other in our digital age is not face-to-face, but online. Far from passive consumers of media, we pay close attention to every new update or article or newscast, stockpiling proofs for every argument that might be raised against us. Every interaction is about our future strategy. Whether the subject matter is politics, religion, race, education, health, or otherwise, everything we focus on or consume in digital spaces is interpreted through the lens of how it might help our team win.

I find myself doing this so often. Before I hit "share," my hand dangles over that "post" button, and I'm maneuvering in my mind, trying to figure out all of the ways that what I'm saying can be taken the wrong way, or all of the ways I'll leave myself vulnerable if I don't account for every possibility. My focus is ping-ponging over the place, sorting through the various scenarios I need to anticipate. My heart has mixed motives: I want to glorify God, but right alongside that is my desire to ensure I am the victor, should an argument break out. Is that how you feel sometimes too? Like you need a personal Public Relations manager just to share a basic thought? Like your attention is constantly darting around through the various ways you'll be perceived? Like you need to come up with a seven-point strategy for being the winner in the conversation, should someone misunderstand or even challenge you?

It's exhausting.

And, as he so often does, Jesus offers rest. His words cut through the noise of such earthly concerns with countercultural, heavenly wisdom. So far we've seen that this wisdom includes poorness of spirit, mourning, meekness, and so on. And now Jesus adds something that will further mark us as a citizen in his kingdom and also help us wisely navigate our interactions with media and with other people: "Blessed are the pure in heart, for they will see God" (Matt. 5:8).

Pure in heart.

There is something so guileless about this phrase—something so counterintuitive when we're plopped in the middle of a culture at war.

The Road to Purity of Motive

To be pure, the *Oxford Dictionary* tells us, is to be "not mixed or adulterated with any other substance or material" or "without any extraneous and unnecessary elements." "Free of any contamination."[1] And *Oxford* isn't alone in this rendering. As it turns out, the Bible had that same definition long before the dictionary did. To be "pure" in both the Old and New Testaments means to be unmixed, uncontaminated, or without blemish.

As believers, we know that, in a biblical sense, purity does not come naturally to the descendants of Adam. Isaiah reminds us that even our purest works are "filthy rags" (Isa. 64:6 NIV). Paul expands upon this oft-quoted verse when explaining total depravity in Ephesians 2:1–5 (ESV):

> And you were dead in the trespasses and sins in
> which you once walked, following the course of this

---

[1] https://www.lexico.com/en/definition/pure

world, following the prince of the power of the air, the spirit that is now at work in the sons of disobedience—among whom we all once lived in the passions of our flesh, carrying out the desires of the body and the mind, and were by nature children of wrath, like the rest of mankind. But God, being rich in mercy, because of the great love with which he loved us, even when we were dead in our trespasses, made us alive together with Christ—by grace you have been saved.

He points out that our issue with purity isn't just our actions, but within our very *nature*—hardwired into our bodies and our minds as it is with every other man and woman on this planet and has been since Adam and Eve ate the forbidden fruit at the serpent's behest. In other words, every component of our human makeup—our heart, soul, mind, and strength—has been touched and tainted by the Fall, contaminating what was once perfect with sin. Being impure doesn't just mean doing some wrong things every now and again; no, it means being compromised from the inside out. It means we are divided instead of whole, focused on many other idols instead of singularly focused on God, mingled with sin on the motive level instead of unmixed, dead instead of alive.

When we see this truth about ourselves, it's clear, then, that the path toward purity is paved not with our good intentions, but with Christ's. As the passage says, God, "being rich in mercy, because of the great love with which he loved us, even when we were dead in our trespasses, made us alive together in Christ."

In a move that echoed millennia of the pure and perfect animals the Israelites were called to sacrifice to atone for their sins, God sacrificed his perfect, sinless—pure—son on behalf of his undeserving, sinful—impure—children.

Transcendent Purity

The conversation about purity of heart starts not, then, with the inherent impurity of our hearts, but with the transcendent purity of the God that we serve. He stands apart from his creation as the very definition of purity—holy, set apart perfection. In the noise of everything that battles to hold our attention and divide our heart—that noise being especially loud in the media—he is the whole, undivided, uncontaminated, unmixed, holy, set apart, *pure* One.

While we battle on the two-dimensional chessboard of our day, our God sits in the heavens in another dimension entirely, transcending the bickering of his temporal creation. In true, transcendent purity, he is undefiled by the war of words that flies back and forth below him, unhampered by the disparate motives that scream for our attention. As the Holy God of the universe, his motive is always purely that: the glorification of himself. Nothing else mixes in with his motives, distracts his attention, or taints his focus.

And nothing else should taint ours.

The first question of the Westminster Shorter Catechism offers us insight into the purity of heart—purity of focus—required of the Christian life.

> **Q:** What is the chief end of man?
>
> **A:** Man's chief end is to glorify God, and enjoy him forever.

It sounds so simple: have a heart that seeks simply and solely to glorify God. Do not take your eyes off of him. Do not veer to the right or the left of the call for him to be your chief end and your primary focus. Do not have a heart mixed with idols, trying to serve God and them at once, nor a heart that tries to focus on both heavenly and earthly concerns at the same time.

His Perfect Example

We already have an example of the single-minded purity of heart and focus that God requires of us in the person and work of Christ—the very speaker of this command.

The night of his crucifixion, Christ chooses a handful of disciples to go with him to the garden of Gethsemane to pray. Though fully God, he is also fully man, and he realizes that the flesh that he is wrapped in is about to face the greatest pain ever meted on mankind. Jesus shows us that single-hearted focus is costly—so costly, in fact, that he weeps tears of blood and says, "My Father, if it is possible, let this cup pass from me. Yet not as I will, but as you will" (Matt. 26:39).

Jesus' surrender here is so complete that he willingly sacrifices himself when Judas brings the great crowd to take him to trial.

His surrender is so complete, that when Peter takes matters into his own hands and wields his sword to chop off the ear of one of Jesus' assailants . . . Jesus intervenes.

> "Put your sword back in its place because all who take up the sword will perish by the sword. Or do you think that I cannot call on my Father, and he will provide me here and now with more than twelve legions of angels? How, then, would the Scriptures be fulfilled that say it must happen this way?" (Matt. 26:52–54)

Though Peter's focus *seemed* to be on the business of Christ—protecting the Savior of the world from bodily harm—his view was too myopic. In fact, Jesus even warned Peter about this very thing earlier in Matthew's Gospel. When Peter hears of Jesus' fate—when Jesus tells him point blank that it was his destiny to be killed and then rise again—Peter says, "Oh no, Lord! This will never happen to you!" Jesus' response is telling: "Get behind me, Satan! You are a hindrance to me." Why? "Because you're not thinking about God's concerns but human concerns" (Matt. 16:22–23). In other words, Peter's focus wasn't pure, meaning, it wasn't singularly set on heaven's agenda and heaven's way of winning. It was divided, mixed, interested in heaven's wisdom to some degree, but trying to make room for earth's agenda and earth's way of winning too. And because his focus was divided, because his heart was trying to mix earthly wisdom and heavenly wisdom, Peter couldn't see that bodily harm was a fulfillment of the Scriptures. Christ would die so that we might live. Jesus understood what Peter missed in his zeal: that God's plan involved surrender, not a drawn sword.

Pure in Heart . . . Online

We can be like Peter sometimes, can't we? Acting like a citizen of the wrong kingdom, focused on the wrong thing? We do this a number of different ways, I'm sure, but we especially do this when it comes to media. We may not be bearing a literal sword when we flip on the news or open our favorite social media app, but we can certainly bear a metaphorical one. Like Peter, our motives are very clear: I want to win. We are guided by the same status-quo wisdom he was, burdening ourselves with the concerns of the world: How can I support my preconceived notions, how can I destroy my opponents, how can I anticipate enemy fire and launch an attack right back?

It should be no surprise to us, though, that keeping God—his glory, his agenda, his concerns, his ways—at the center of our focus is difficult for Peter and for us. Adam and Eve lived in a perfect garden where their every want was satisfied, and they were *still* caught off-guard for temptation. How much more for us who are so very far removed from Eden, with myriad iterations of the serpent calling out to us from every screen?

The command *sounds* easy enough: to be pure in heart, our heart's focus must be on God above all else. But the inevitable question is, what does that *look* like?

What does that look like when vigilantes storm the Capitol and we're wondering who's to blame? What does it look like when our economy is being crippled by a worldwide pandemic and we don't know the way out? What does it look like when battle lines are being drawn in the sand in our communities, in our families, in our churches?

What does it look like to be singularly focused on God *without* putting our heads in the sand?

Here is where the beauty of Christ's words slice through the noise, if we listen to them:

Blessed are the pure in heart, *for they will see God.*

Blessed are those whose hearts have a single-minded focus on God, because he will reveal himself to them. Or, said another way, the kind of person whose heart has been purified from a million other focal points is the person who gets to behold God. Jesus' heavenly wisdom is so simple and true: you cannot see God when the eyes of your heart are darting everywhere else, looking for things you think are more alluring. The heart Jesus is talking about here is one that has been wiped clean of all those idols which once jockeyed for attention, and what does that leave behind? A now undivided, laser-focused heart—one that is no longer on a swivel, but is forever turned toward the thing it wholeheartedly seeks without anything tainting the view: God. It sounds so obvious when we think about it, doesn't it? When the eyes of a person's heart are purified from other things to focus on, and solely focused on God, *she will see him.*

In Jesus' kingdom, every citizen gets to see God because every citizen has a heart that wants to look at him. Problem is, we have hearts that like looking elsewhere (media being one of many examples). So how do we get the kind of heart that Jesus is talking about? Hebrews 11:6 (ESV) states that "And without faith it is impossible to please him, for whoever would draw near to God must believe that he exists and that he rewards those who seek him."

Faith is the cornerstone of this heart-purity—the faith to take our eyes off of the overstimulating twenty-four-hour news cycle and pin them to the cross. The faith to believe that God really is a better, more interesting, more alluring thing to behold than that anger-inducing headline or that fiery quarrel everyone is gawking at. The faith to trust that knowing and glorifying God is better than winning an argument. The faith to know that our answers lie, not in the carefully choreographed arguments of the online opponent for which we have the most affinity—but in a God whose battle for us is not even *about* flesh and blood (Eph. 6:12). The media can tell us a lot about the flesh-and-blood dimensions of this battle we're fighting, but it can tell us very little about the spiritual battle God's children are engaged in.

And how will we *know* how to fight?

He has told us: in his Word.

We will constantly find ourselves in a state of desperate squinting if we're looking for God anywhere other than his Word. Our hearts will be forever mired in the impurities of this world if that's the only diet we are imbibing. Only through a consistent steeping in the Word of God can we hope to be pure in heart and focus in our unfocused world.

The question for us, then, is not whether or not we should care about the headlines happening in our culture. Of course we should. The question is this: What is the state of our heart when we engage with them? What is our affection and our focus set on when we navigate conversations around these things? Would we say we are *wholly* and *purely* fixed on God and his glory and his ways? Or is our motive mixed? Furthermore, we'd do well to ask this too: Are we lingering to take in God in his Word *far more often* than we linger around those headlines and fiery disputes? Are we setting our heart and attention more on him than on winning? If the answer is yes and yes, then we will still care about the latest culture war, yes, but *the way we handle it* will change, for our focus will be wholly set on God's glory, his victory, and his ways of winning instead of our own.

The Truly Pure in Heart

In a world constantly vying for our attention, to linger on the Lord in such a singularly focused way is quite challenging. Instead of going to Jesus to really take him in, on *his* terms, finding out what it means to be a citizen that rightly represents *his* side in this world, we would *much* rather Jesus just come down and tell whichever political or digital opponent is getting under our skin that he's actually on *our* side.

But to look at the sides we're presented on this two-dimensional chessboard is to misunderstand the fact that we serve a God who transcends every petty squabble. And the answer is not crippling defeat of our enemies in the here and now—but suffering service on behalf of our king who will reward us so much later than we'd often like to think.

Whether we see them on a social media post, an article, an interview, or a newscast, what if we actively chose not to see other believers as opponents to be destroyed, but rather brothers and sisters—family members in Christ to be loved and encouraged? What if we took more comments offline and out of the ambiguity of a meme or a hot take and into the kind of deep, meaningful relationships that Jesus modeled with his disciples?

It sounds scary, doesn't it? Going about our digital conduct this way—or *all* our conduct, really—leaves us vulnerable. It doesn't put us in the winner's seat in the social media fray.

But here's the best news: when we find ourselves mired in the vicious cycle of media consumption—when we find our hope drowned out by the noise of a constant input of information from our phones, laptops, and television screens—when we find that our hearts are far from pure, but rather, mired in the filth of these earthly battles . . .

We have a King named Jesus who stands ready to intercede on our behalf. He has done it perfectly. He has walked this earth with a single-minded focus: the will of his Father. He did that so he might become the perfect, atoning sacrifice for the impure children whom God had chosen, and so that, by his blood, we would stand before the Father, blameless.

This exercise in focusing our minds and hearts on God and his great gospel is an important piece of sanctification—the journey by which we are becoming more and more like Christ every day. *And* when we fail—because we will inevitably fail—we can praise him for having already been perfectly pure in heart on our behalf. And the even better part? As we do this—as we go to him in the moment of failure, confessing that our focus has shifted once again from his eternal victory to our petty and temporary "wins," as we seek him and ask him to reorient our focus and purify our hearts from all the other things that jockey for our allegiance, we *actually do* become purer in heart over time. When we turn from the things dividing our heart or pulling at our focus, and seek him, he will reveal himself to us and in doing so, change us.

He truly does think of everything.

Application

Looking In

Take some time to take inventory on the state of your heart and focus. Use these questions to help you:

1. If you could describe your conduct in digital spaces these days, how would you describe it? Do you ever maneuver your way through social media interaction like it's a game you have to win? How would it feel to focus, instead, on glorifying God and loving others with what you post?

2. We all consume the media in some form or fashion. Which type of media makes you the most angry, or starts to shift your motive toward winning instead of glorifying God?

3. Why do you sometimes assume that a catchy headline or an online squabble is a more interesting thing to behold than God?

4. If you're leading other Christians, do you think your conduct online would be a good example for them to follow when it comes to being pure in heart? Why or why not?

Looking Up

Now that you've taken time to examine your own heart, shift your focus off of yourself and fix it on the Lord, who does not leave you to yourself in this place, but helps you and teaches you.

1. Jesus is the best example of what it means to be pure in heart—what are some examples of the singular focus of his ministry on the earth?

2. In what ways do you, like Peter, tend to prize the battle here on earth more than you prize Jesus' priorities?

3. How often do you come to God and confess your distracted, divided heart, and ask for his help to purify your focus or motives? How often do you ask God to help you fight battles according to heaven's ways instead of the ways of earth? Why do you think this is the case?

Looking Out

Consider purity in heart on a broader level than just the way it plays out in your own life. Zoom out, and think through how it might impact the world around you if you leaned into it more often.

1. As you look out at our broader culture, do you see evidence of unhealthy engagement with media? Why do you think this is happening?

2. How can you use your social media interaction to encourage others to look to Christ alone?

3. How can you stop playing the endless chess game and start digging deeper into real relationship with Christians who might disagree with you on certain issues? What would it look like for you to engage in civil dialogue with those folks, making space for deep conversation? (And if you did this, how might that change the assumptions non-Christians make about Christians?)

4. How might you help your small group or Bible study grow in purity of heart, especially in digital spaces?

Looking Ahead

As you look forward to the new heavens and new earth, where Christ will reign forever in glory, consider how purity in heart helps point to that coming kingdom.

1. In both digital and in-person conversations, what would the world around us assume about Jesus' kingdom if all his followers were fully focused on glorifying God? What conclusions would non-Christians draw about Jesus if his people entered into fiery battle zones according to heaven's wisdom instead of relying on the tactics of earth?

2. When you imagine Jesus' kingdom coming in full one day, how does purity in heart play a role?

Prayer of Confession and Commitment

Dear Lord, I confess to you that I have taken my eyes off your will and your ways. I confess that I have behaved a bit like Peter in the garden, wielding the sword of my tongue (Prov. 12:18), instead of surrendering to whatever your will may be for me, trusting in the wisdom of earth instead of heaven. I ask that you guide me to the knowledge of what will truly glorify you, and not myself. I ask that you would help me to be about kingdom work and kingdom ways of handling the fighting that goes on all around me. I pray that you would give me the singular focus of Jesus in the garden, even when it hurts. I pray for the purity of mind, thought, and action that can only come from you—the Most High God—through the blood of your Son, Jesus Christ. Amen.

Chapter 8

MAKING TRUE PEACE IN A WORLD OF FALSE PEACE

Rachel Gilson

*"Blessed are the peacemakers, for they
will be called sons of God."*
—Matthew 5:9

Have you ever tried to settle an issue in a well-meaning way, only to realize later down the line that you didn't handle things very well? Have you ever stood up for the right thing, and suddenly found out you were utterly wrong?

Consider Jane Austen's classic *Pride and Prejudice*. Whether you prefer the BBC version, Keira Knightley's, the classic novel, or a combination of all of them, we've all fallen in the "Mr. Wickham" trap. We fully side with main character Lizzy when she rejects Mr. Darcy's first proposal because, like her, we have heard all about his nastiness from sweet Mr. Wickham and have seen ourselves Darcy's obvious conceit. What's more, we feel proud of Lizzy for how she rebukes his arrogance and cruelty. She has spoken the truth, kept her honor, and shown him what's what. Only through time and pain does it become clear that Wickham is the scoundrel, and Darcy the man of honor. Lizzy is able to change her course before it was too late, to great relief and a happy ending.

We in the church have some courses to change ourselves, before it's too late. When it comes to peacemaking, we've too often skewered our Darcys while standing in defense for our Wickhams. And the same could be said for much of our attempts to make things right; our peacemaking so often falls short of what it could be.

Sometimes we do nothing, because trying to make peace is risky, scary, or exhausting. Sometimes we attempt to make something right, and it blows up in our faces.

Peacemaking can be so tricky, and yet Jesus said, "Blessed are the peacemakers, for they will be called sons of God." In a world that is just fine with staying at war with itself, and even *enjoys* all the fighting we see going on around us, Jesus reminds us that those who do the work of making peace are the ones who not only truly flourish in this life, but prove themselves to be genuine "sons" of God. If we want this kind of flourishing,[1] then, we can't look to the world around us, to social media, or to our own instincts. We have to look instead at *the* Son of God, the Prince of Peace, and follow him.

Look to Jesus

If there were a heat map in the Bible to show us how to find lessons on Jesus and peacemaking, one of the reddest spots would hover over Ephesians 2:14–16:

> For he [Jesus] is our peace, who made both groups one and tore down the dividing wall of hostility. In his flesh, he made of no effect the law consisting of commands and expressed in regulations, so that he might create in himself one new man from the two, resulting in peace. He did this so that he might reconcile both to God in one body through the cross by which he put the hostility to death.

---

[1] For more on the concept of the Beatitudes as ways of flourishing in life, see *The Sermon on the Mount and Human Flourishing: A Theological Commentary* by Jonathan T. Pennington.

Let's double-click on the lessons of this passage and learn from Jesus, the Master, about what real peacemaking is.

Peace Received

The very first thing we need to get from this text is that before God ever calls us to *make* peace, he calls us to *receive* peace. We will flourish when we act like Jesus in the world, amen. But we can't begin to walk on that path of flourishing while we're still a corpse on the road. Jesus is our peace; it doesn't come from us. If it weren't for his life, death, and resurrection, we would be stuck forever as God's enemy, and as enemies of one another. See, Scripture says we were once at war with God, him on one side, us on the other. But because of the mediating gospel work of Jesus, the two sides are now at peace with one another (Col. 1:21; Rom. 5:1, 10). Which means we have to lay down any pretensions we have of being "all right enough" to go this on our own, as if we merely need Jesus to put the finishing touches on all the good things we do. No, every drop of our peace with God comes from him, for the amazing price of *free*. We just have to humbly open up our arms and take it.

Eternal Peace

Once we've received peace, we can start thinking about making peace. After all, you can't give something that you don't own. One of the most important things we see about true peacemaking is that it prizes the eternal; it is always going to run to fixing that which will last forever. The beginning of Ephesians 2:16 says, "He did this so that he might reconcile both to *God*." That is, Jesus did all of the work mentioned in the passage (which we'll explore below) so that people could be forever reconciled to an eternal God. His goal was to mend a once-broken relationship that was going to last forever. If we were to get from Jesus a sort of quick-fix peace in our daily lives, perhaps getting our toddler to stop crying or getting our neighbor to finally agree with us about the boundary lines of the yard, and yet miss out on life with the eternal God now and forever, we would have only won a temporary victory. Like being in the lead most of a game, only to lose the championship in the last moments. The loss is what lingers.

If we set our sights on working for peace, we do well to keep our minds on making the sort of peace that will last forever. That certainly means inviting people to hear the good news of salvation through Jesus Christ, so that they might believe and come into his family and live eternally with him! Jesus died and rose again so that this offer might be received by anyone who would believe.

But what about those short-lived situations? Does our view of eternal life and peace have to crowd out all other types of peace that Jesus cares about as well? Are there other types of peace, here-and-now ones, that matter to him?

Indeed. Jesus came preaching *and* healing *and* feeding (and sorting out squabbles within his own followers). Why? Because though the bread and fish lunch for 5,000 didn't last forever, he knew the *people* who ate that meal would last forever. Every human is made in God's image, and deserves dignity, honor, and value because of that. There is not a single human who is not precious to God. This is why we want each person to receive forgiveness and forever peace! It is also why temporary types of peacemaking have value as well. How we treat image-bearers, crying toddler, disgruntled neighbor, and even enemy alike, reveals how highly we view the One whose image they bear (Matt. 25). And on top of that, these small, temporary attempts at making peace act as little pictures, pointing the world to the God who extends the chance to be at eternal peace with them in Christ.

Reconciling Peace

This brings us to the second thing we learn about peacemaking from Ephesians 2:14–16: while the primary goal is eternal peace with

God, a secondary result that Jesus' work brings about is a "here and now" peace between groups of Christians as well.

And it's not just a stalemate kind of peace, an absence of obvious fighting while everybody is still raging mad at each other. That picture is more like high schoolers thrown into detention together because they were brawling in the hallway. They're not throwing punches anymore, because they're sitting under the eye of a teacher, but anger is still bubbling and brewing inside. That is "peace" in only the most superficial way.

No, instead, our passage says that Jesus "made both groups one" and that he "create[d] in himself one new man from the two." The picture here is that same group of high schoolers going from side eye to side hugs. The peace is so thick that they aren't primarily two different groups anymore, even though differences remain. They are more truly one group in Jesus, brought together like one body, with Jesus as the head. The concept the Bible uses for this sort of thing is not just peace, but *reconciliation.*

While the gospel has the power to reconcile those who have all sorts of differences, our passage here in Ephesians specifically has two groups in mind, the Jewish people and everyone else who wasn't Jewish, known in the Bible as Gentiles. God had kept the Jewish people whole and separate to prepare the world for Jesus, who was the long-awaited One who would turn all the promises God had made to the Jews into *Yes* (2 Cor. 1:20)! But God also meant for the whole world to get in on promises that were fulfilled in Jesus. While there was good purpose for Jewish identity distinction, the big plan was for that blessing to spill over onto everyone else.

God has done this; he has made his church a collection of both Jews and Gentiles. In fact, we are a collection of all kinds of peoples. If we belong to Jesus, then we are meant to experience reconciliation and family relationship with all other types of people who also belong to him, whether we are gathered at our local church, or we encounter fellow believers in other environments. My favorite personal experience of this was at the seminary I went to in downtown Boston. My classroom was regularly filled with Africans, Caribbeans, Koreans, Chinese, Brazilians, as well as Americans of these backgrounds as well as others. We were all there to learn more about our God. We are not called to lose our heritage or our culture, but to be at peace with each other in those beautiful differences, unified as brothers and sisters under our King and Savior.

Jesus doesn't just create peace across ethnic or racial lines, of course. He makes peace across every boundary that exists, for those who trust in him. We see this even in his inner circle during his ministry. One of his followers was literally named Simon the Zealot, because he at some point had been dedicated to overthrowing Roman occupation of Israel. Yet another one of his followers was Matthew, a tax-collector, someone who *participated* as a Jew in Roman dominion, and made money off of it. Politically, it doesn't get more divided than that. Yet both of these men were called by Jesus, and transformed by him too. We don't get to hear about how they navigated their different political opinions, yet we see them unified because they both followed Christ.

Fighting for Peace

But let's be real, because the Bible certainly is. Just because two people believe in Jesus with their whole hearts doesn't mean they will experience peace with each other.

Twice in our passage, the word "hostility" shows up. In verse 14 it says that to make peace, Jesus "tore down the dividing wall of hostility" that existed between the Jews and Gentiles. And notice the actual violence of the peacemaking in verse 16: "He did this so that he might reconcile both to God in one body through the cross by which he put the hostility to death."

Jesus put the hostility between Jew and Gentile, the hostility between God and humanity to death; he killed it dead, by submitting to death himself. To follow Jesus here truly requires wisdom.

On the one hand, we learn that some peace is only gained through a fight. This is why we call it "peacemaking"—there's an assumption it is not already there and has to be *made*. We flourish when we attempt such peacemaking, but it doesn't come easy. If it did, so much of our weariness would already be dealt with. Instead, we have family feuds that last decades. We have theological wars that go on for centuries. We have lingering distrust between black, white, Asian, and Latinx churches. We have friendships that fall apart in our hands. We stubbornly refuse to listen to some of God's commands, preferring the ones we're already comfortable with. None of these nor any other type of relational conflict will disappear without painful, hard work.

Now, don't get me wrong. The fact that we have to fight for peace doesn't mean we fight like the world does. No. We reject violence in the fight of personal peacemaking, or any tactics that deal in evil. Peacemaking for the Christian won't involve lying, manipulating, or caving before sin. Nor will it mean throwing tantrums or harming others. To make peace means to rejoice with what is good, to abhor what is evil, and to test everything against the supreme value of love. That means we never ask of others what we aren't doing ourselves. Even when it will cost us.

Sacrificial Peace

After all, Jesus came to make peace, and he was murdered for it. His body was torn so the walls could be torn down. He was targeted because he called out the practices of the spiritual leaders that dishonored God and dishonored image-bearers. He was taken down because he preached repentance, and meant it. He promises that peacemaking is the way toward the good life for the believer, but paradoxically, peace also requires a heaping dose of selflessness.

If we become peacemakers, it will require words and actions that make us, and others, deeply uncomfortable. Not uncomfortable in the cute-awkward way we talk about it sometimes. Uncomfortable like telling your dear friend who is considering an abortion that a little human life is still a human life, no matter how small that life is. Uncomfortable like telling your racist uncle at Thanksgiving that his joke at the expense of other humans isn't funny. Uncomfortable like examining your own heart honestly, your own dismissiveness or divisiveness toward others.

The sad truth is we've made false peace with our messes. When we are at odds with someone else, we've refused to genuinely assess if we have a log in our own eye before we go pointing out the speck in someone else's (Matt. 7:5). We've said it's not really our fault, or said "what-about-so-and-so," on and on, to protect ourselves from the discomfort required to deal with the places *we* might be the problem in the conflict. Peacemaking is costly, which is why we don't do it even though we know we should, kind of like that gym membership we bought but don't use. Jesus' peacemaking was costly, and it was not a cost he owed. He would have been perfectly fair and just to let us remain in our sin, separated from him. But because of the great love with which God loved us, the Father sent, and Jesus willingly came, emptying himself of that which was rightfully his. It is no surprise then that our own peacemaking attempts will require a setting aside of things we deserve, or things we like and aren't wrong to have. The peace the Bible talks about must be selfless and sacrificial, because like love, it is always thinking of the other person's good.

Revealing Peace

Blessed are the peacemakers . . . do you remember the rest? Don't worry, this pop quiz won't show up on your transcript. But what *is* the blessed truth about the Christian peacemaker in a world full of fighting? Blessed are the peacemakers, *for they will be called sons of God.* The Christian peacemaker, before God, has a status, and with that status, a name.

When we are united to Jesus by faith, God begins to transform us so that we look more and more like him. And who is Jesus, exactly? A son. Think about it. In the Trinity, he is God the Son (Rom. 1:3). In his ministry, his favorite term for himself was the Son of Man (Matt. 16:13–15). Two of the four Gospels spell out his genealogy, tracing his sonship. Son of Abraham, the man of faith (Matt. 1:1–2). Son of David, and his true heir (Matt. 1:1, 6). Son of Adam, come to undo his ancestors' disaster (Luke 3:38). Though many true and beautiful titles belong to Christ Jesus, Son is one that rings out like a wedding bell, like the trumpet of a triumphant parade. He is the Son who imitates his glorious Father, and we are to imitate him. Especially in his work of making peace.

When a child comes into a family, she takes the family name and begins to learn the family ways. Children can resist this process, but even those of us who grew up *so annoyed* by that tone of voice our mom used can one day find that same tone coming out of our own mouths. We can't help it. After all, kids act like their parents. They cannot remain unaffected. They pick up on their parents' traits, their value system, their ways of operating in the world, their approach to handling threats or enemies, and so on. As they walk in this world, people look and immediately recognize the family they belong to. "Oh there goes so-and-so—she has the same mannerisms as her dad!" The same is true for the family of God, in which we are the children and God is the heavenly parent. If we are already sons of God, his children, that seed of making peace is there, waiting to be tended, waiting to bear fruit. Said another way, if we are God's children, and God is a peacemaker through Christ, it follows that as we walk in this world, we'll do what he does. When we do what he does, it will reveal whose we are. Blessed are the peacemakers, for they will be called sons of God.[2]

---

[2] You might notice that the language of "sons" is sex-specific. Does that mean that girls or women are cut out of this picture? Not at all! The language of "sons" is used for Christians because in the context in which Jesus spoke, sons were the children who had the right to inherit all that belonged to the father of the family. By calling us "sons," God is encouraging us that we are each his full, legal children, entitled to an inheritance because of Jesus' work on our behalf. (Remember, too, that the church is called the bride of Christ, another sex-specific image that in no way cuts out male Christians from the joy of intimacy with their Savior.)

False Peace, False War

In closing, we need to look at actions that camouflage as peace-making but aren't.

The first one is *false peace*. This is when we don't address a sin or situation with another party that must be addressed. False peace can happen on the individual level, like when our friend is using social media in ugly and unhealthy ways and we refuse to gently challenge her on it. Or it can happen on the communal level (or even the church level), when we turn a blind eye to things like abortion or racism or sexual abuse.

When we are tempted to ignore something because it's hard, or risky, or "not my problem," this is right where we need to be on guard against false peace. This is where we remember what we learned above: sometimes peace involves a costly, sacrificial, eternally minded fight. And if we're only fighting when something directly impacts us, that's not selfless or sacrificial, and therefore not a sign of Christlike peacemaking.

This leads us right into a different danger: *false fights*, which claim to be waged for the sake of peace, but actually work against it.

One type of false fight is when something is good, but not ultimate. For example, there really is a right way to load the dishwasher (anyone else with me on that?). But even if your spouse or roommate should know that by now, it's not worth attacking them over it. To this, you might say, "Fine, fair. But what about heavier situations . . . like when my reputation is dragged through the mud? Or when I fear what is coming politically for my country?" Things like this do bring out in us a desire to make things right; the question is: How can we press pause and evaluate them?

Here's one way to evaluate it, based on what we learned above: How much overlap is there between the good thing we want to fight for, and forever things? The less connection there is, the more likely we are to be spending our energy on false fights. And the more a thing really is good, yet still not forever, the more likely we are to get deceived. The more a thing stirs up our fears and our passions, the more we need to double-click, look hard, and not assume.

There is a second kind of false fight too. This is when we've got the right cause but the wrong target, or perhaps the wrong execution. One example of this has been how the church has handled the topic of sexuality in our culture. When there *is* something worth fighting for regarding sexuality, are we sure we're aiming at the right target?

The Bible is so clear about the danger of sexual immorality, and the beauty of faithful singleness and faithful marriage between one woman and one man. And church folk, in their good desire to prize such teaching often warn others at length about the cultural dangers "out there" that fly in the face of said teaching—things like the commonness of sex outside of marriage or society's celebration of same-sex relationships. Yet for all our warnings about the types of sexual immorality that exists "out there," we can neglect versions of it that happen "in here"—meaning, *inside* the church.

For example, most churches do not have sexual harassment policies set up in their congregations. Yet sexual harassment or abuse in the church is just as much a violation of God's good design for sexuality as any other sin. Or who isn't aware of yet another spiritual leader caught in adultery or abuse, all while preaching conservative sexual ethics in their pulpits? Or consider a final example: when it comes to entertainment consumption, many believers will change the channel on an LGBT+ love story in a sitcom, yet are fine with watching heterosexual sex scenes, reading explicit romance novels that arouse lust in the mind and heart, viewing internet pornography, or entertaining the idea of adultery when connecting online with an old high school sweetheart.

The God of the gospel blesses sexual purity and even commands it, but only the God of the gospel can provide it. When we care about something like sexual purity, we care about a good thing. But too often a so-called concern for sexual holiness has actually played out in shaming, excluding, and judging people outside the church, the ones *not* claiming to follow Jesus, while turning a blind eye to our own massive sins, the ones who claim to follow him! We must repent in accordance with Paul's teaching in 1 Corinthians 5:12–13: "For what business is it of mine to judge outsiders? Don't you judge those who are inside? God judges outsiders. Remove the evil person from among you."

The fight for sexual purity is just one example of many things worth fighting for. It's important. But let's ensure we are keeping the proper target in mind—namely, sin that is running amok in God's household. Because sons and daughters act like their family members, and our big brother Jesus aimed squarely here.

In conclusion, peacemaking does sometimes require conflict, but that heavy truth must be soaked with wise discernment. Are we fighting for the right things? Is our primary target to purify "the culture," or is our primary target the church, which God has actually called to holiness and harmony? And when we do seek to make peace with those outside the flock of God, are we attacking people, or are we attacking the sin that enslaves them? God help us.

Look to Jesus

Jesus told his followers, "The one who believes in me will also do the works that I do. And he will do even greater works than these, because I am going to the Father. Whatever you ask in my name, I will do it so that the Father may be glorified in the Son. If you ask me anything in my name, I will do it" (John 14:12–14). Jesus is sitting with the Father right now, eager to give us what we need to be called sons of God. In a world that constantly wages war for all the wrong reasons and in all the wrong ways, the work of making peace in a Christlike way is sometimes costly, sometimes confusing. But we are God's children, and he is not stingy, nor poor. He is ready and waiting to give us all the wisdom we need to flourish in our work of peacemaking. And when we do, we bear one mark of what it means to be not only his kingdom citizens, but his kids.

Application

Looking In

In order to become peacemakers, we have to identify a few things. First, we must evaluate whether or not we've indeed received the kind of eternal peace with God that Ephesians 2 talks about. If so, we need to identify if we have not been living as if that's true. Or in other words, we need to identify where we have been picking false fights, hitting false targets, or keeping a false peace.

1. Have you received the peace with God that comes through Christ's reconciling work on the cross?

2. Which section of this chapter felt most encouraging to you? Which section felt most challenging or convicting? Why?

3. How open are you to critique on what you fight for? Or, on the flip side, when you know you should make peace with someone, but avoid it and refuse to engage, what do you think is holding you back?

4. Where have you been peacemaking according to worldly wisdom? Where have you waded into a false fight, or set your eyes on the wrong target? Where have you been "keeping the peace" in a strained or broken relationship instead of directly handling the issue you know you need to deal with?

Looking Up

God is the ultimate peacemaker, and longs for us to be his true sons. He sees our pettiness, our cowardice, and our laziness, and he is ready not only to forgive us when we confess and repent, but to give us wisdom and power to make his peace.

1. The best time to repent is always now. What false fights or false peace have you participated in that you can you bring before God today, asking for forgiveness and help?

2. Take some time to read and study all of Ephesians 2 with friends, or alone. What do you notice about how God made peace? What were his attitudes and motivations? Who did it impact? What steps can we imitate, and which can God alone do?

3. Take some time to remember your own conversion story. In what ways were you at war with God? How did Jesus forge peace between the two of you? How does his example influence the way you forge peace in your own relationships?

Looking Out

Peacemaking, among all the Beatitudes, is one of the most outward-facing. By God's strength, we can make real peace now.

1. What are some worldly ways of "making peace" that you see in our broader culture, and do you think they've found their way into the church? Why do these methods fall short of true peacemaking?

2. "Therefore, since we have been justified by faith, we have peace with God through our Lord Jesus Christ" (Rom. 5:1 ESV). The greatest gift of peace we can offer someone is the offer of peace with God through Jesus Christ. Who are some people who don't know God that you can pray for, and share your faith with? When it comes to your skills in sharing the good news of the gospel, if you don't feel trained, where might you seek training?

3. Consider your family, your friendships, your church, your community. Where might God be calling you to pray and move toward peace

even now? Pray that God would give you wisdom, and talk with other Christians.

4. If you lead other Christians in a group, consider the state of your group. Are there any needs for members to make peace with one another? Is there any evidence of false peace or false fights? How might you help lead your group toward greater health in this area?

Looking Ahead

Making true peace with others today points to the perfectly peaceful world that will one day come in full and last forever. Consider these questions to meditate on this reality:

1. Read Isaiah 9:6–7. How does this passage give you hope for future peace as believers await the new heavens and new earth?

2. Reflect on how the Lord's Prayer empowers and directs the work of peacemaking:

> Our Father in heaven,
> your name be honored as holy.
> Your kingdom come.
> Your will be done
> on earth as it is in heaven.
> Give us today our daily bread.
> And forgive us our debts,
> as we also have forgiven our debtors.
> And do not bring us into temptation,
> but deliver us from the evil one. (Matt. 6:9–13)

Prayer of Confession and Commitment

Father, though I was once your enemy, you made peace with me by the blood of your Son's cross—thank you! Help me to make peace with others according to the wisdom of heaven and not earth. Give me discernment to know when something is worth fighting for—and when the time comes to enter in a certain conflict, help me do so in a sacrificial and Christlike way, therefore revealing myself to be a child of yours. Remove any sin in my heart that is causing problems with those inside or outside the church, help me aim for the right target when I fight for important issues, and give me eyes to see any false versions of peace in my relationships. Amen. 🔥

Chapter 9

PERSECUTION IN A WORLD OF COMFORT

Mary Wiley

"Blessed are those who are persecuted because of righteousness, for the kingdom of heaven is theirs."
—Matthew 5:10

"Hey! Don't cuss around Mary. She's a Christian."

I shifted in my plastic blue chair as my gaze became glued to the stained carpet of my high school's band room. This was shortly before I learned that my reputation as a Christian also kept me from knowing about the parties that happened on the weekends and the latest drama everyone was whispering about in the lunchroom.

I felt canceled before "cancel culture" became part of our vocabulary. I wanted to be respected and "in the know," and it seemed all the cool kids were careful to shield me from the knowledge of what was happening on the weekends because I spent a large majority of my weekend at church.

It was years before I realized this wasn't persecution, but was actually God's kindness to me to protect me from my not-fully-formed teenage brain that would probably not make the wisest decisions had I not been shielded. I remember feeling embarrassed as I read through stories of martyrs or suffering in the global church due to their faith in Christ. My experience wasn't really suffering, and I wasn't ever even insulted, but I was so quick to assume any amount of friction the resulted from my faith was persecution.

It was as if I had a persecution complex—so adverse to the smallest discomfort that might result from following Christ, that I assigned it the title of persecution so I might at least receive Jesus' promised blessing for my maladies.

If I'm honest, I still prefer to avoid suffering at all costs. I don't even want an acquaintance I haven't spoken to since high school to unfollow me on social media, but the truth is, I've never experienced persecution for following Christ. Not in the way the Bible paints it. Misunderstood, avoided, or deemed unloving, sure. But never persecuted. Because of where I live, I have full religious freedom and freedom of speech. Honestly, from a global and historical standpoint, I have a really comfortable situation compared to so many others.

So how should we think about persecution as those who rarely face it today?

Wisdom Explained

In what is arguably Jesus' most beloved sermon, he lists the traits of those who walk wisely in the world. As you've already read in the previous chapters, these are the blessed: the poor in spirit, those who mourn, the meek, those who hunger and thirst for righteousness, the merciful, the pure in heart, the peacemakers, and the persecuted. We could spend our entire lives asking the Holy Spirit to make these true of us and still have miles to go. Each instruction holds implications for both the inward working of the heart and the outward working of our lives, but this one leans heavily upon the right response to sure outward attacks as followers of Christ.

> "Blessed are those who are persecuted because of
> righteousness, for the kingdom of heaven is theirs.
> You are blessed when they insult you and persecute
> you and falsely say every kind of evil against you

because of me. Be glad and rejoice, because your reward is great in heaven. For that is how they persecuted the prophets who were before you." (Matt. 5:10–12)

I imagine the crowds looking around to catch eye contact with those who may have traveled with them to hear this great teacher. *Persecution? Insults? Is that what we sign up for if we choose to believe and follow this Jesus? No, no, no—that can't be right. I thought he was ushering in a mighty kingdom!* Yes, he did say he was ushering in a kingdom, but this kingdom doesn't belong to the strong. As this book has pointed out already, it belongs to the poor in spirit and the persecuted—the insulted and the mistreated.

Jesus, in his all-knowing kindness, spoke words of preparation for those who were listening. Soon, if not already, they'd face persecution. They'd look loved ones in the eye who didn't understand why they would leave everything to follow Christ, and they'd face the mocking of their Rabbi as he was led to the cross to be crucified. If his people were living in line with the countercultural instructions before this one, they would be easy to identify and easy to misunderstand or misrepresent. After all, the way of the cross seems absurd to those who do not believe (1 Cor. 1:18).

And yet—God's kingdom belongs to these. This is the kingdom Jesus proclaimed in Mark 1:15: "The time is fulfilled, and the kingdom of God has come near. Repent and believe the good news!" This is the first recorded statement from Jesus in the book of Mark, and it seems Mark is intentionally revealing its importance. The kingdom of God has come near through Christ! God the Father has sent the Son as he promised through the prophets, and he is ushering in a new kingdom that is *already here,* but at the same time, *not yet fully here.* It is ushered in through Christ and displayed, furthered, and manifested by the church as we wait upon its full realization at his return. Many Jews awaited the coming Messiah because they thought he would restore the kingdom of Israel, and yet throughout Jesus' ministry he reveals he was bringing not an earthly kingdom (Mark 10:15), but a better, eternal kingdom.

In Jesus' crucifixion, he was mockingly declared "King of the Jews" with a crown of thorns upon his head. Those crowning him would not see the ways God was revealing him as King, even in these moments of greatest suffering until later, with some never grasping the irony of the mockery being the greatest truth. In Jesus' resurrection we see him welcomed as victorious over sin and death, insults and persecution, and in his ascension we see a coronation as he sits down at his rightful place at the right hand of the Father, reigning eternally.

We are first citizens of this kingdom Jesus ushered in. No other allegiance, nation, tribe, group, or shared interest unites and applies identity like God's kingdom. We are his agents tasked with manifesting his kingdom in the world, or revealing God's character and mission in the way we live. The beauty of the kingdom today is the presence of God with his people and the good, holy reign of Christ that is both, as I said before, already and not yet. This is the worthy prize and the promise to the one who faces suffering for the cause of Christ and perseveres—the one who faithfully lives with open hands, welcoming whatever may come, even if it hurts.

The Way of the Cross

Around AD 200, as Christians suffered great persecution under the Roman Empire, an influential early church father wrote the following: "The blood of the martyrs is the seed of the church."[1] Under the most tortuous of emperors, the church experienced explosive growth in both number and faithful commitment. Imagine being under the leadership of the Emperor Nero who particularly enjoyed impaling Christians and placing them in his garden as torches to light the night simply because of their commitment to Christ. Yet, the result of Nero's

[1] Tertullian, *Apologeticus*, L.13

persecution wasn't the snuffing out of Christianity, as he had hoped. The result was Christianity spreading like wildfire.

This time in the life of the early church is not divorced from Paul's call just 150 or so years earlier to submit to authorities in Romans 13, an instruction found within a book that defines gospel living and calls us to the way of the cross—which is the way of death-to-self and suffering. While submitting to authorities, we still hold in mind that our citizenship is not of this world. Submission does not mean complete passivity, but it is an open-handed obedience to the authorities when it can be held in harmony with submission to Christ, and a willingness to face the legal consequences when this can't be true. In Christ's example, we do not see him lashing out or arming himself against those who insult or mistreat him; instead, we see gentleness and care and a willingness to face whatever may come. This is the surrender to which we are called.

But what does this look like for us?

The Bible gives us many examples, two of which are found in the book of Daniel. King Nebuchadnezzar built a huge idol of gold and decreed that all would bow down to it when they heard an instrument play (Dan. 3:1–6). Yet, Daniel's friends were steadfast, refusing to bow. They answer the king's questioning and promise to throw them into the furnace in verses 16–18, "Nebuchadnezzar, we don't need to give you an answer to this question. If the God we serve exists, then he can rescue us from the furnace of blazing fire, and he can rescue us from the power of you, the king. But even if he does not rescue us, we want you as king to know that we will not serve your gods or worship the gold statue you set up." God delivers them from the fire, and Nebuchadnezzar is moved to believe "there is no other god who is able to deliver like this."

Wow, right? Similarly, Darius decrees that no one can pray to any god except to the king himself for thirty days (Dan. 6:6–9). Daniel is seen praying to the one true God and is brought before the king. You know how this story ends. He is thrown into the lions' den, suffering the consequences of his commitment to God, and God shuts the mouths of the lions (Dan. 6:10–23), which leads to Darius declaring Daniel's God as the One who should be worshiped!

Beyond Daniel and into the New Testament, when we point to our heroes of the faith who have handled persecution well, we watch in wonder while they find such joy in Christ that the external situations of their lives are but a momentary inconvenience and an opportunity to preach Christ and him crucified to an audience. They are not like the plant that springs forth without a root in the parable of the sower, quickly falling away when persecution comes (Mark 4:17). No, standing steadfastly in their hope in God, no matter what may come, is the mark of the Christ-follower, and it is this faith that may lead the persecutor to belief!

I pray I would be more like Daniel and his friends than this plant without roots. The fruit of our lives reveals the condition of our hearts, and as trials and testing come, we bleed what is already inside. Will we choose the way of the cross: gentle, sacrificial, and ultimately simply seeking to glorify the Father? Right obedience to the call of Christ is foolishness to those who don't believe (1 Cor. 1:18), and if we do it well it will certainly be misunderstood, misconstrued, and mocked. If the crowds treated our sinless Savior this way, surely we will face the same as those who do sometimes misspeak, misstep, or misrepresent Jesus, but may we count these trials as great joy because it matures us in Christ (James 1:2–3). These can be considered blessings because we are joining the faithful prophets before us in a large cloud of witnesses for Christ.

Matthew 5:10–12 is written in the literary form of *chiasm*, or a sandwich of truths, with Jesus at the center. The beginning and end mirror each other, as the persecuted are called blessed and also are put among the faithful who have also experienced persecution for the sake of righteousness. As the structure builds inward, we find the reward is heaven in both verses 10 and 12. The key of a chiasm is usually in its center, and in this particular teaching, we find Jesus there. He's the grounding point of this passage. He is ultimately what the persecutor reviles, and it is his image within a person that brings about the insults and hatred.

Jesus does not say, "You are blessed when they insult you and persecute you and falsely say every kind of evil against you because of your political stance" or "because of your take on the state of Christianity in America" or "because of your view on a certain culture war." Instead, he says, "because of *me.*" Peter would remind us of the same in his letter when he tells us that we can call it persecution—and we can believe blessing is ours—when we are persecuted *"for the name of Christ"* (1 Pet. 4:14, emphasis added).

We may get unkind remarks from friends in our neighborhood (or perhaps on our social feeds) when it comes to all of those things above, and that may make us feel uncomfortable or insecure or worried. But none of that qualifies as persecution in the way Jesus is defining it here in the Beatitudes. Persecution means you are harmed simply for believing in Christ, bearing his name, and walking like him in this world.

The faithful have been persecuted since the advent of the church and it is an honor to suffer with Christ just as the prophets before us. It is an honor to take on Christ's life, death, resurrection, and ascension as those united in him. There is never a time when we outgrow or graduate from suffering as Christians. There is no promise of a pain-free, comfortable life in Scripture and no promise that following Christ will result in health, wealth, or prosperity. The Christian doesn't avoid trial nor can a Christian escape the painful realities of a fallen world that the Enemy has woven into our society through his ministry of whispering lies and inciting sin.

This is the overwhelming promise of the New Testament. In this life you will have trouble (John 16:33), yes, but we can live in the midst of that trouble as those enjoying citizenship in a better kingdom with a promise of a better eternity. This has been the lifeblood of the saints since the very beginning.

Grasping for Security

How did the Roman Empire identify Christians in its midst so that it might persecute them? Righteousness. The Christians were living righteous lives in line with the character of their righteous Savior. And that's the same righteousness for which we strive today. Yet if we're honest, our struggle is this: the decisions we make in everyday life sometimes point not to our seeking of righteousness, but to our seeking of security and comfort.

> We prioritize our jobs and paying off our mortgage so that we might be financially secure or at least comfortable.
>
> We avoid even necessary and biblically grounded conflict in favor of secure, comfortable relationships.
>
> We obsess about our diet and our health hoping that it will keep our bodies free from disease.
>
> We overprotect our children, thinking we can keep them insulated from hardship or the grief that comes from it.

While stewardship is a righteous endeavor, security and comfort above all else is nothing short of idolatry, deeply rooted in fear. For example, consider election season. It's not hard to see that fear runs through communities of faith on both sides of the political aisle. Some of us feel afraid we may be losing some semblance of power, authority, or sure path toward justice. Others of us are afraid that losing means persecution for our faith is inevitable. Still others of us are scared because we feel entitled to a world that agrees with our belief system and allows us to practice our faith without any opposition.

Jobs, friendships, health, kids, election cycles—these are all just examples. But the truth in all of it is this: earthly security is and has always been a mirage. It's fleeting, and as soon as you feel like you can grasp and hold it, it has moved another mile from you. Our world is ever-shifting, and the algorithms required to land on top change day-to-day. We pander after health, wealth, and prosperity, reaching for them as some measure of God's favor, and yet they cannot hold our weight. There is no security apart from Christ, and the loss of whatever idea of earthly security we have for the cause of Christ is not the worst thing that could happen to us. In Christ, we have eternal security, the only lasting comfort.

May we not be like Peter who says, "I don't know him," in an attempt to save ourselves some suffering (Luke 22:54–62). May we ask the Holy Spirit to root out our idols and embolden and strengthen us to do God's will. And if we walk so closely with Christ that it brings suffering, may we find deep joy in the great reward that awaits.

There is beauty in placing our security squarely where it belongs, in that God is the only One who is strong enough to hold it. A rightly placed security frees us to both use our influence in the public sphere wisely, while not feeling as though the world is ending if the religious freedom we are fighting for feels like it's slipping through our hands. The call to Christlike living is not a call to be a doormat or to seek out pain for pain's sake, but it is a call to rightly place our commitment to Christ and to loving our neighbor above our comfort. If this commitment puts us at odds with our ruling authorities, all right, come what may. Our security is not and has not been in a particular outcome, but a particular Person all along.

So what does rightly placed security look like? It is only when our feet are securely planted on the foundation of Christ and his work that we may able to do as Paul instructs in Romans 12:14: "Bless those who persecute you; bless and do not curse." This counterintuitive response is the outworking of the Holy Spirit, a response that leaves the onlookers astonished. It is in the response of Daniel and his friends, who welcomed the trial and revealed to Nebuchadnezzar and Darius the power of their God, bringing many to faith. It is in Jesus' prayer to his Father as he is nailed to a cross, "Father, forgive them, because they do not know what they are doing" (Luke 23:34). This is the way of the cross, the upside-down kingdom of God.

Christlike suffering like this—the type of suffering that is impossibly compassionate, even to the point of death—doesn't make sense to those who are without the Holy Spirit. To those of us who are indwelt by him, suffering is seen as a gift when it comes as a result of righteousness.

Storing Up Joy for Days of Trouble

Suffering is a gift, albeit a difficult one to receive. We stand on the shoulders of giants of the faith who prove that suffering produces much fruit in bringing glory to the One we hail as King. Are we committed unto death? Are we prepared to "boast in our afflictions, because we know that affliction produces endurance, endurance produces proven character, and proven character produces hope" (Rom. 5:3–4)? Can we trust that "this hope will not disappoint us, because God's love has been poured out in our hearts through the Holy Spirit who was given to us" (Rom. 5:5)?

Persecution isn't new, and it isn't ending. A report on the global church from Open Doors UK states that in 2020, there are 260 million Christians suffering under high levels of persecution for their faith in the top 50 countries on their World Watch List.[2] As recently as 2015, the US experienced a shooting at the Emanuel African Methodist Episcopal Church. Suffering is promised, but so is the kingdom as the reward for righteous endurance. Increased persecution may mean a leaner church and a separation of wheat and chaff, but it will also mean a stronger, truer church. May we live righteous lives that are worthy of insult because of our unnatural, unexpected, heavenly response when the world seems to be on fire. Let us walk in the way of the cross with open hands, knowing that this might hurt. I pray we consider it joy, willing to be injured because we know the Binder of our wounds.

---

[2] Open Doors UK and Ireland, https://www.opendoorsuk.org/persecution/wwl20-trends/.

Consider it a great joy, my brothers and
sisters, whenever you experience various trials,
because you know that the testing of your faith produces endurance. And let endurance have
its full effect, so that you may be mature and complete, lacking nothing. (James 1:2–4)

Application

Looking In

1. Where might you be tempted to place your security?

2. How have you responded when others have insulted or belittled you? Are there examples that are directly related to your commitment to Christ?

3. If someone was evaluating your life, would there be enough evidence to warrant persecution on behalf of your life?

4. How might you live a more open-handed, even-if-it-hurts life?

Looking Up

1. How might you better rely on God as your joy giver when you face suffering?

2. How might you ask God to prepare you today for persecution that you may face? Spend some time praying that he would give you the strength and boldness needed to proclaim the gospel in both word and deed, no matter the cost.

3. How might you ask God to realign your priorities today so that your commitment to Jesus would be the leading characteristic of your life?

Looking Out

1. What might it look like to encourage others as they face persecution?

2. How might we celebrate and join in praying for those who are standing firm in the face of persecution around the world?

3. What might it look like to be a community of people of faith so committed to Christ that your life would be foolishness to those who don't believe?

4. What does it look like practically to bless those who curse you?

Looking Ahead

1. As Christian values increasingly become considered "foolish" to the world around us, persecution and insults toward those who would seek to walk in the ways of Christ can be expected. How can you store up joy today for coming days of trouble?

2. What does it look like to live as a local church (or a small group, if you're a leader) who is collectively prepared and strengthened for any coming persecution?

3. Imagine what God's kingdom looks like in the return of Christ. Why is this picture worth living for, even if it comes with temporary pain from those who don't hope in it?

Prayer of Confession and Commitment

God, we are weak and so conditioned to prefer our earthly security and comfort over your kingdom. We praise you with our lips, but often deny you with our lives, and we ask you to forgive us. May we live open-handed, even-if-it-hurts lives that honor and glorify you. We pray our lives would leave those who do not know you astounded and confused because of the joy and devotion they see in us. We are committed to you and to the work you are doing to further your kingdom as we await your glorious return! Amen. 🔥

Chapter 10

SALT AND LIGHT IN A WORLD OF DECAY AND DARKNESS

Jen Pollock Michel

"You are the salt of the earth. . . .
You are the light of the world . . ."
—Matthew 5:13–14

In the eleventh grade, Molly sat behind me in American history. I was a new Christian, eager to make good on the commitments I'd made at summer camp: to pray and read my Bible every day; to share my faith, every week, with a nonbeliever. That year, Molly had a target on her back.

I faithfully looked for ways to turn my conversations with Molly toward spiritual topics. I mentioned spending time at youth group. I dropped the name of Jesus as frequently as I could. When our church held a revival service, it's obvious whom I asked.

Molly did agree to attend a couple of services. I don't remember much about those services except the experience of sitting next to Molly each night as the sermon wound down and the music piped up, calling sinners forward. My palms sweaty, my head bowed, I prayed as fervently as I could to move Molly from her seat—but she never budged.

Those early years as a new believer carried real zeal for the Lord, and I'm grateful for that. But they also carried a few regrets too, one of them being the way I handled my relationship with Molly. I hate admitting how she was my pet evangelism project. Now, don't get me wrong; I certainly think a Christian should seek to share the gospel. But that wasn't the issue with Molly. The issue was that, to me, she was a problem to solve, someone to merely convince and convert—and I didn't even succeed in doing that. As a new Christian, I didn't understand the kind of influence I might have exercised in Molly's life, nor did I have a full picture of what being a Christian "witness" meant. My intentions were good, but my understanding was limited.

Wisdom Explained

The Bible gives us a much richer vision of our relationship to the world than we often conceive. It's certainly a more fruitful, faithful picture than "target" for our "gospel bombs." In fact, our relationship with our irreligious neighbors is one that requires imagination, which Jesus engages in the Sermon on the Mount with his comparisons of "salt" and "light." These are metaphors, or words at play. Instead of giving us a three-step process for convincing and converting our neighbors, Jesus invites us to "taste" and to "see" how we might faithfully love him by loving his world.

Jesus' hearers would have made immediate connection to "salt" and "light." These object lessons connected them to the features of their land. For those traveling from the region of Galilee, they might have thought of the town of Magdala, which was on the western shore of the Sea of Galilee. This was the center for salting and preserving fish.[1] Just to the south, in the region of Judea, salt was in plentiful supply, washed up on the shores of the Dead Sea (also called the Salt Sea). Salt was common in every household, necessary to prevent food from rotting. It seasoned, preserved, and purified.

Jesus' disciples might have also thought of the ancient Decapolis city, Hippos, located on the eastern shore of the Sea of Galilee. Set

---

[1] Barry Beitzel, ed., *Lexham Commentary on the Gospels* (Bellingham, WA: Lexham Press, 2018), 139.

up on a hill, it was a luminous Roman city with temples, bathhouses, gymnasia, and other cultural buildings. As one commentator explains, Hippos shone the light of Rome on the surrounding region. It was a city that was visible, even glorious.[2]

When Jesus compares his followers to the *salt of the earth* and the *light of the world*, there are many things we might learn. The first thing to notice, of course, is that there is a relationship between the church and the world. These words cast a vision of the church's influence *by proximity*. It's a mission that requires a certain degree of nearness. Salt, to do its work of preserving, curing, and flavoring, must actually touch food like fish and meat. Light, to do its work of illumination, must shine in a dark room. Salt in a jar or a lamp under a basket cannot do the job they've been made to do. Their effectiveness depends on contact.

Simply put, as gospel salt and light, we cannot live God's call from our cozy, Christian bubbles. We can't light our lamps inside church walls and hope the light spills into city streets. We can't throw salt over the neighbor's fence in hopes of seasoning their burgers. We can't love the Mollys of our lives from a few chairs over without engaging the willingness to understand their questions, their longings, their fears, their hopes. We must be visible, active, engaged in our neighborhoods and communities, exerting influence through proximity and relationship.

In fact, this is exactly how God himself cast his light (and shed his salt) into our world. Instead of staying at a safe distance, as the apostle John wrote, God "became flesh and dwelt among us" (1:14). He moved into the neighborhood, as Eugene Peterson would say. He walked the streets of this world. The disciples "tasted" and "saw" the glory of God through Jesus, and now Jesus commands his followers: let the world "taste" and "see" my glory through you.

The world cannot be loved from afar.

---

[2] Ibid., 140.

The Struggle

Rightly, many of us worry about the negative influence of the world, should we pursue any kind of "friendship" with it (1 John 2:15–17). Here's where we must deepen our understanding of the nature of salt and light.

As salt, God's people *prevent* decay. As we live out the upside-down nature of God's kingdom as outlined in the Beatitudes, we provide an uncompromising witness of moral clarity and courage in the world. Our meekness, our mercy, and our love for righteousness—our embodiment of the Beatitudes as we go about our days—challenge the world's self-serving ideals. God's people proclaim truth—and also live it. Their witness is one of both word and deed, and it can be decidedly unpopular.

But this isn't to say that the stance of Christians is always *against* the world. As light, we *promote* truth, beauty, and goodness. As God so loved the world, we long for the world's repair and redemption. We are not of the world, but we are in it—and emphatically *for* it. The world may remain hostile to the Christian, but the Christian lives as Christ: "When he was insulted, he did not insult in return; when he suffered, he did not threaten but entrusted himself to the one who judges justly" (1 Pet. 2:23). Because Christians have somewhere, rather some*one*, to whom we can take our suffering, persecution loses its power to stifle our love for the world.

In these four verses, Jesus is helpfully orienting our expectations of the world. The world is decaying. The world is currently a realm of darkness, and when Jesus, the light of the world, entered this darkness, it refused him welcome (John 1:10–11).

It's popular today to pine for some lost era of American history, but Jesus reminds us that the world we inherited, post Genesis 3, has always been a broken, sinful one. When the flaming cherubim swords drew and Eden's east gate closed behind Adam and Eve, the only world we've known is one that is turned against God. Every person, every family, every nation has gone astray like lost sheep (Isa. 53:6). This is not cause for despair or fear or hand-wringing, but a reminder that in this story God's scripting through history, we find ourselves today in the middle act: the world, not as it once was, the world not as it one day will be.

The decay and darkness of the world is not cause for surprise. And yet, it's real cause for struggle.

How do we live in a decaying, dark world? How do we maintain our saltiness, which is to say our distinctiveness? What will our relationships with the world really look like—in our neighborhoods, online, in the public square—especially in this cultural moment, when the Christian voice seems increasingly marginalized and unwelcome?

We might be tempted to walk in one of two directions.

Some Christians, throughout history, have chosen the path of cozy conformity. In fear of ruffling the feathers of the world, they've abandoned the counterculture to which they are called, and as a result, they inevitably embrace every whim of their culture without much thought. This is to say that they have failed to cling to the realities of "sin, righteousness, and judgment" (John 16:8). They forget the world is a system steeped in sin. They fail to proclaim the saving work of Christ. They neglect to see and preach the fearful truths of eternity. They can be of no real good to the world because, as the late John Stott put it, they lack the bite of true salt, the heat of true light.[3]

Other Christians make another kind of mistake, walking down the path of easy escape. Not wanting to be polluted by the world and constantly offended by the reality that it is fallen, they fail to love it. Their posture toward the world is one of fear, even one of hostility. Although their Lord has laid down his life for this world, seeking to save it, their witness is one of contempt and condemnation. Their only language is one of protest. Their only position is one of opposition. They, too, can be of no real good to the world because they will not risk the nearness to sinners that love requires.

---

[3] John Stott, *The Message of the Sermon on the Mount* (Downers Grove, IL: IVP, 2020), 48.

To be clear, the call to be salt and light requires us to engage something more complex than an either/or. It requires that we do not swerve from truth a single inch, in any one direction of compromise. We must not compromise on truth—and we must not compromise on grace (John 1:17).

It can be helpful to read how Jesus prayed for us to uphold this tension in our lives:

> "I have given them your word, and the world has hated them because they are not of the world, just as I am not of the world. I do not ask that you take them out of the world, but that you keep them from the evil one. They are not of the world, just as I am not of the world. Sanctify them in the truth; your word is truth. As you sent me into the world, so I have sent them into the world . . . so that the world may know that you sent me and loved them even as you loved me." (John 17:14–18, 23 ESV)

Jesus prayed for his people to be sanctified—and also sent. He prayed we would be grounded in truth—and also commissioned by love. He prayed we would reject worldliness—and also love the world for his sake.

Testifying to the Gospel

The good news is that Jesus, our elder brother, has carried on this gospel mission of truth and grace, of salt and light. He is our example, and his Spirit is our power. God's firstborn son emptied himself, becoming obedient to death on the cross that we might have *his blessing*.

Blessing is the gospel current running through the entire Bible. It was a blessing that Abraham was called both to receive and also to give away to the nations (Gal. 3:8). We might remember the picture of

Jacob, Abraham's grandson, on his deathbed, in Genesis 49. Before he took his final breath, he blessed his sons, and we might imagine Jacob's hands stretching across the centuries, resting through Jesus on our heads.

We might remember that we now are the hands and feet of Christ, stretched out with love toward God's broken world.

The Beatitudes have given us a vision of being the blessed people of God. We are invited into the fullness of joy that is Christ's. There is nothing to protect, to hoard, to worry because we stand to inherit the earth. We will see God. We have received these blessings—and as salt and light, we look to give them away to the world. Isn't that something? Where we would settle for heavenly wisdom that helps us *survive* or, at best, *navigate* a world at war with itself, Jesus empowers us to do something all the more rare and beautiful and unexpected: to *bless* it.

Like the prophets of God, who are both mentioned before and after this short selection of verses calling us to be salt and light, our blessing of the world is not a baptism of niceties. We don't bless the world as it has blessed itself, allowing itself to think, "I will have peace even though I follow my own stubborn heart" (Deut. 29:19). No, we bless the world by reminding it that sin is the rot and ruin of our lives, that Jesus rescues us from the way that once seemed right to us, though it led to death. We bless the world by remaining deeply rooted in the Bible, which tells us the truth about ourselves, the truth about the world, the truth about our need for rescue, the truth of our Savior.

What This Might Look Like Practically

Ten years ago, our family moved from Chicago to Toronto. Some people call Toronto the most cosmopolitan city in the world, meaning that it draws people from every corner of the globe to make a home here. In Toronto, we're half-immigrant, half native-born. But this city is worldly in another way. As a whole, it rejects the truth of the gospel. It does not see its sin, and it does not see its need for a Savior. In fact, the proclamation of sin—and salvation through Christ alone—are often received as primitive, even dangerous ideas.

My friend works as a physician at a local hospital and describes herself as someone more committed to science than spirituality. Raised in a mainline Protestant church, she married a Jewish man and raises her children with hybrid religious commitments and identity. She aggressively supports abortion and physician-assisted death. She worries aloud that Christian opposition to homosexual practice and gender transition makes our LGBTQ+ teenagers vulnerable to suicide and homelessness.

To say that my friend and I disagree on many political and social issues is to understate our radically different ethical systems and starting points. She believes human beings flourish when they follow their own earthly desires. I believe that we flourish when we submit our lives to our heavenly Father and Creator—and follow his Christ.

These differences can be cause for tense conversations, but our friendship is surviving them. Unlike my more insecure days with Molly, I make no apology for being a Christian, even for wanting my physician friend to become one. Instead of simply praying for her, I've even prayed with her. Instead of forcing her on my turf to hear about the Bible from the pastor, in ordinary moments of our everyday conversation, I regularly let her in on the truths I'm learning from the Bible and what it looks like to be shepherded by God in my life. Very clumsily, I try to live out the radical call of salt and light, of grace and truth. I don't ignore the differences of our beliefs, but I try staying in relationship with her, try remembering that God's mission is one of proximity, try reminding myself that what gives spiritual conversations their saltiness and radiance is a whole life lived around them, a life lived in the ways and wisdom of the posture of Christ, who as the Beatitudes show us, seeks to bless. I never get it exactly right, which is never the point.

God's mission is enacted by God's Spirit, and every new birth is an event of grace.

In ancient times, new babies were often rubbed in salt (Ezek. 16:4), which lends yet another dimension to Jesus' words at play as we think about the nature of Christian mission in the world. I want my friend to be born again, rubbed in the salt of gospel grace, and I know this will only be possible when the wind of God's Spirit blows (John 3:5–8). It will only be possible when "God, who said, 'Let light shine out of darkness,' has shone in our hearts to give the light of the knowledge of God's glory in the face of Jesus Christ" (2 Cor. 4:6). God is the giver of salt and light, and he has so loved the world that "he gave his one and only Son, so that everyone who believes in him will not perish but have eternal life" (John 3:16).

I want God to give me his own self-giving love for the world, a love that was so apparent in the ministry of the apostle Paul. He felt a "great sorrow and unceasing anguish" for the world's decay and darkness: "I could wish that I myself were cursed and cut off from Christ for the benefit of my brothers and sisters" (Rom. 9:2–3). Paul would have traded his gospel inheritance of blessing for the curse of the lost.

I don't yet know this level of love for the world—but I want to.

Application

Looking In

It's helpful, before we move into action, to examine our attitudes toward the world. Before we consider being salt and light, we also need to consider our attitudes toward decay and darkness.

1. What is your stance toward the world: fear, hostility? Cozy conformity or easy escape? Cowardice or Love? Why is this your default stance?

2. How have you previously understood your identity as salt and light? What new insights have you gained?

3. When you think of your witness in the world, which of the Beatitudes is most challenging for you to live out in your relationships?

4. What prevents you from being in relationship with people who don't know Christ? Busyness? Indifference? Worry about their influence over you or perhaps your children? Lack of gospel conviction, that without Christ, they are eternally lost?

Looking Up

This passage reminds us that mission, as God's people, is rooted in identity. We aren't simply called *to do*. We are called *to be*. Being rightly related to God rightly orients us to the world he loves and seeks to save.

1. Think about God's prodigal grace in your own life, back before you knew the Lord. In what ways were you unworthy of God's love and help? In what ways did he reveal himself as "salt" and "light" to you in that place of decay and darkness?

2. What passages in Scripture call to mind the gospel current of God's blessing? Where do you see evidence in those passages of the "both-and" nature of this blessing, that it stands against sin and stands for sinners?

3. What transformation can you seek by the power of God's Holy Spirit? Have you lost your saltiness? Have you refused your responsibility to shed light in the world? Do you lack desire to see God glorified in the world?

Looking Out

It's helpful to remember that God's mission is right under our feet. We often don't have to look far to identity the people God is placing in our lives to whom we might minister his truth and grace.

1. What is one relationship you can begin cultivating as you respond to the call to be salt and light?

2. Instead of merely "convincing and converting" this person (or group of people, if they came to mind), how does the word *blessing* change your understanding of your movement toward them?

3. Are there other opportunities for involvement in your children's school, in your neighborhood or community, or in your local government that would give you opportunity to prevent decay and promote good? What small step can you take toward that opportunity?

4. If you lead other Christians in some way, consider the group as a whole. Does your group lean more toward cozy conformity or easy escape? Why? How might you collectively pursue being "salt and light" in healthier ways together?

Looking Ahead

Mission in the world requires us to see it as a team sport, not a solo performance. The mission of God belongs to the church. It also requires us to have a very long vision of reality, to see this world, this earth, is only one short chapter in God's time line. We need to be people who cultivate a sense of the eternal.

1. How can you remain as hopeful about the mission of the church as Jesus was, that he is "glorified in [us]" (John 17:10)?

2. What are some specific ways you can help yourself remember that the work of the kingdom is slow, small, and often imperceptible? How can this encourage you when you don't see immediate fruit from your efforts to love the world? Is there anyone else around you who might need you to encourage them in this truth as they are laboring for the kingdom?

3. What passages of Scripture give you a vision of eternity, holding you steadfast in courage and hope, even when the world remains hostile to you? What are some creative ways to keep those passages in front of your eyes more often?

4. When the world feels like it's up in flames some days, what will help you keep living out the Beatitudes in your daily life? What does living this way show a world on fire?

Prayer of Confession and Commitment

God, I confess that I don't see the world as you see it, that I don't love the world as you love it. I thank you for the mission that you've entrusted to your church, and I thank you for your commitment to glorify yourself through us. Help me to live out my calling to be the salt of the earth and the light of the world as I endeavor to embody the Beatitudes. Help me be faithful to the wisdom of heaven, even when it feels upside-down on this earth, all for your name's sake. Amen.

ABOUT THE AUTHORS

Hannah Anderson is an author and Bible teacher who lives in the Blue Ridge Mountains of Virginia with her husband, Nathan, and three children. Her books include *All That's Good: Recovering the Lost Art of Discernment and Turning of Days: Lessons from Nature, Season, and Spirit.* She also cohosts the *Persuasion* podcast, which addresses cultural, theological, and more mundane issues from a Christian perspective. Hannah's goal is to encourage believers to think deeply and broadly about how the gospel transforms every area of life.

Jada Edwards is a Bible teacher and discipler. She has committed her life to equipping women of all ages, at all stages, with practical, biblical truth to help them live authentic and transparent lives. Jada has always had a passion for ministry and sharing God's Word and has served in various directional capacities within the local church as well as with numerous nonprofit organizations. Jada holds an MBA with an emphasis in Organizational Strategy, but her most significant education has come from the study of God's Word. The unsearchable riches of the Scriptures are her inspiration. In addition to her ministry in the local church and her teaching ministry, Jada works with Caribbean Choice for Christ, a U.S.-based nonprofit leadership organization, founded by her and her husband, Conway. Their ministry focuses on developing and equipping Christian leaders throughout the United States and Jamaica. Jada currently serves as the Creative Services Director and the Women's Director for One Community Church, where Conway serves as the Lead Pastor. Jada and Conway are parents to Joah and Chloe, and live in Allen, Texas.

Rachel Gilson (MDiv) serves on the leadership team of Theological Development and Culture with Cru, and is the author of *Born Again This Way: Coming Out, Coming to Faith, and What Comes Next* (The Good Book Company, 2020). Her writing has appeared in *Christianity Today* and for Desiring God and The Gospel Coalition, and she speaks nationally and internationally at churches and on college campuses. Rachel is pursuing a PhD in public theology at Southeastern Baptist Theological Seminary, and lives in the Boston area with her husband and daughter.

Ashley Marivittori Gorman serves as an associate publisher at B&H Publishing Group, an imprint of Lifeway Christian Resources. She holds an MDiv from Southeastern Theological Seminary and has been trained under The Charles Simeon Trust. Her passions are biblical literacy, women's discipleship, foster care, theology, books, and teaching the Bible. Ashley and her husband, Cole, live in Nashville, Tennessee, with their daughter, Charlie. You can find her writing in various Lifeway Women Bible studies, in books like *World on Fire*, and in digital venues like The Gospel Coalition, Lifeway Voices, the ERLC, Relevant, and Intersect Project.

Jasmine Holmes is the author of *Mother to Son: Letters to a Black Boy on Identity and Hope* and her forthcoming book *Carved in Ebony*. She is also a contributing author for *Identity Theft: Reclaiming the Truth of Our Identity in Christ* and *His Testimonies, My Heritage: Women of Color on the Word of God*. She and her husband Phillip are parenting two young sons in Jackson, Mississippi.

Rebecca McLaughlin holds a PhD from Cambridge University and a theology degree from Oak Hill College. She is the author of *Confronting Christianity: 12 Hard Questions for the World's Largest Religion* (2019), *10 Questions Every Teen Should Ask (and Answer) about Christianity* (2021), and *The Secular Creed: Engaging 5 Contemporary Claims* (2021).

Jen Pollock Michel is the award-winning author of *Teach Us to Want, Keeping Place* and *Surprised by Paradox*. Her fourth book, *A Habit Called Faith*, released in February 2021. She holds a BA in French from Wheaton College and an MA in Literature from Northwestern University. An American living in Toronto, Jen is a wife and mother of five. She is the lead editor for *Imprint* magazine, published by The Grace Centre for the Arts. You can follow Jen on Twitter and Instagram @jenpmichel and also subscribe to receive her letters to readers at jenpollockmichel.com.

Mary Wiley is the author of *Everyday Theology*, an eight-week Bible study exploring essential doctrines and why they matter in our everyday lives. She holds a BA in Christian Studies and English from the University of Mobile and an MA in Theological Studies from The Southern Baptist Theological Seminary. She and her husband, John, have three children and live in the Nashville area. You can follow her @marycwiley.

Elizabeth Woodson is a Bible teacher, writer, and speaker, who is passionate about communicating the rich theological truths of Scripture. She loves helping people internalize their faith and connect it practically to everyday life. Elizabeth works as the Institute Classes and Curriculum Director at The Village Church in Flower Mound, Texas, where she teaches classes on the Bible, theology, and spiritual formation. She formerly worked as the Single Life Coordinator at Oak Cliff Bible Fellowship under the leadership of Senior Pastor Dr. Tony Evans. Elizabeth is a graduate of Dallas Theological Seminary with a Masters in Christian Education and a cohost of the podcast *Culture Matters*.